EXAMINATION

OF THE

PRINCIPLES AND POLICY

OF THE

GOVERNMENT

OF

BRITISH INDIA

EXAMINATION

OF THE

PRINCIPLES AND POLICY

OF THE

GOVERNMENT

OF

BRITISH INDIA

BY A GENTLEMAN
(HENRY DUNDAS ROBERTSON)

GYAN

Published by

GYAN

Gyan Publishing House
5, Ansari Road
Daryaganj, New Delhi-110002
Phone: 011-47034999, 9811692060
E-mail: books@gyanbooks.com

Distribution Network
gyanbooks.com
India, USA, Canada, UK, Australia

ISBN: 978-81-212-7053-3 (PB)
First Published, 1829

2nd Impression 2024

Printed at: Gyan Press, Delhi.

EXAMINATION OF THE PRINCIPLES AND POLICY OF THE GOVERNMENT OF BRITISH INDIA

Author: A GENTLEMAN (HENRY DUNDAS ROBERTSON)

EXAMINATION

OF THE

PRINCIPLES AND POLICY

OF THE

GOVERNMENT

OF

BRITISH INDIA

EXAMINATION

OF THE

PRINCIPLES AND POLICY

OF THE

GOVERNMENT

OF

BRITISH INDIA

BY A GENTLEMAN
(HENRY DUNDAS ROBERTSON)

GYAN

EXAMINATION

OF THE

PRINCIPLES AND POLICY

OF THE

GOVERNMENT

OF

BRITISH INDIA:

EMBRACING

A PARTICULAR INQUIRY

CONCERNING THE

TENURE OF LANDS;

STRICTURES ON THE ADMINISTRATION OF JUSTICE;

AND

SUGGESTIONS FOR THE IMPROVEMENT

OF THE

CHARACTER AND CONDITION OF THE NATIVES IN GENERAL.

BY A GENTLEMAN

IN THE SERVICE OF THE HONOURABLE THE EAST INDIA COMPANY.

LONDON:

HURST, CHANCE, AND CO.

ST. PAUL'S CHURCH-YARD; AND J. UPHAM, BATH.

MDCCCXXIX.

PRELIMINARY ADDRESS.

THE Author of the following pages has devoted many years of his life to the service of his country in the East Indies, and, having enjoyed access to the best sources of information, he hopes that he shall not incur the charge of vanity in presuming that his opinions are entitled to some attention. The same zeal by which he has been actuated to discharge, to the best of his ability, the duties entrusted to him, for the benefit of all classes of his fellow-subjects, urges him to submit to His Majesty, to his ministers, and to the public in general, those views of the government of British India, which spring from no preconceived notions, which are taken up to support no adopted theory, but which are the result of practical experience and personal observation. If, in the exposition of his sentiments on this important subject, the author has occasionally used what may perhaps be considered strong language, the only excuse he shall plead is, that it is the language of truth: and however disagreeable his strictures may be to some ears, he should have deemed himself culpable to withhold them, deeply as he is impressed with the conviction that our vast Indian empire demands early attention and fostering care, and that, on the foresight and humanity of the measures which shall be pursued in regard to it, depend not only the security and stability of British power in the East, but also the prosperity and happiness of millions.

INDIA,
August, 1828.

BRITISH GOVERNMENT

IN

HINDOOSTAN.

ETC.

It would be a waste of time were I to detain the reader with even a brief sketch of the conquest of India by its present rulers. We are now in possession of that extensive empire, but by what means, or with how much justice, it is the province of the professed historian to relate. In what manner soever our dominion in the East has been acquired, it is a duty incumbent on us so to govern the conquered nations as to ensure to them the greatest possible happiness. Should injustice have been done in any case, this duty becomes the more imperative, for the sake of our own honour, and more especially for the indemnification, as far as it may be practicable, of those upon whom the injustice may have fallen.

I assume as a position which cannot be controverted, that the British Government is determined to maintain the supremacy of India as long as it can maintain it. It has expended its blood and its treasure in the conquest; and its right of domination is thus established, according to the usual notions of mankind. Bearing this in view, the questions to which I wish to draw the attention of the public are,—First, the extent to which the people of India may be permitted by their rulers to become intelligent, and to be raised from a state of indigence and wretchedness to one of comfort and prosperity;—and Secondly, the means of effecting the proposed end.

Reason and humanity dictate that the extent of the improvement that should be allowed ought to be the greatest possible. The difficulty of the problem lies in the just admixture of ingredients to maintain inviolate the fair interests of the two parties; the interests of the conquered, and the interests of the conquerors. So long as the profit derived by the British Government and nation from India is assured by the sword and by religious toleration, any system of Government that may be devised for the nations of that empire by their conquerors will, for a long period, perhaps, be accepted by them. They have no alternative. They possess no advocacy but in the civilization, wisdom, and humanity, of their masters. They are disarmed and have no physical power. They possess freedom of conscience, and are bereft of that strong and manifest rallying point of public sentiment to excite general rebellion, which is to be found in religious intolerance. It therefore rests entirely with his Majesty's Government to ascertain the just proportions of the power and interference to be retained for the maintenance of our supremacy; and of the civil rights, rank, and privileges to be yielded to the nations of India, to enable them to advance in happiness and civilization. If we do this, justice will be rendered to this people; if not, our Government will be considered, and operate as a curse; for if they derive none of the consideration or the benefits of British subjects, they would have been happier under those whom we designate their own tyrants.

The desire of the servants of his Majesty and the East India Company to govern well is indubitable. The anxiety of the Court of Directors and the Board of Controul to better the condition of the people has shown itself on many occasions; and the orders of these public bodies to the local Governments of India are honourable to the British character. But, after all, their care and good intentions have produced inadequate or unexpected results; and how to place the government of India on any thing approaching to an unexceptionable footing is still an unsolved and intricate problem.

Some clever men have assured us that, the more widely extended our power should become, the more would our Government be in danger of subversion; and these authors would of course insinuate, that a civil war would be the means resorted to for accomplishing this end. Authorities of talent and great local information have considered it incumbent on the conquerors of India, if they would retain their sway, to reduce the people to the lowest state of intelligence and poverty, consistent with the reasoning faculties and bodily support of man. I shall examine the views and fears of these legislators, and endeavour to determine how far they consist with sound policy, and the honour and duty of the British nation. At the time this theory was propounded and adopted, we were making long strides towards universal dominion. Another class of politicians, at an earlier period of our intercourse with India, upheld a very different course of reasoning, and endeavoured to create a gentry of landlords. Whatever was the scheme of the day, the end in view invariably was the stability of our power, and the happiness of the conquered people. One might recommend a loyal aristocracy; another, the abolition or suppression of all temporal rank and baronial power, to enable the government, by entering the huts of the peasantry, to proclaim and practice justice, and thus to invite the attachment of the mass of the inhabitants; but, as both were carried away by particular views, adapted to support their own opinions and to oppose all others, the public functionaries at the head of Indian affairs necessarily selected that plan which seemed to present the best arguments for the stability of the British power, and which possessed, though not a real, at least a highly plausible claim to adoption, from its apparent humanity in respect to the people.

The effects of our governing India on those principles are now discernible; and—whether it is that a government of foreigners is inherently depressive to such a people, or that the schemes have failed from a want of attention and care in reducing them to practice; whether the data on which they were founded are fallacious, or have only produced the results anticipated—it is but too true that our East India Government may be justly compared to a noxious vapour, blighting every thing it lights upon.

It is but too certain that the minds of the people are running to waste, and daily approaching nearer to a state of vegetation. But I cannot better or more philosophically describe and account for the condition at which many have already arrived, and to which all others are hastening, than in the words of an eminent writer. "There can be no doubt," says Mr. Mill, "that, by increasing every year "the proportion of the population which you "employ in raising food, and diminishing every "year the proportion employed in every thing "else, you may go on increasing food as fast as "population increases, till the labour of a man "upon the land is just sufficient to add as much "to the produce as will maintain himself and "raise a family. But, if things were made to go "on in such an order till they arrived at that "pass, men would have food, but they would "have nothing else. There would be nothing "for elegance, nothing for ease, nothing for "pleasure. There would be no class exempt "from the necessity of perpetual labour, by "whom knowledge might be cultivated, and "discoveries useful to mankind might be made. "There would be no physicians, no legislators. "The human race would become a mere multitude of animals of a very low description, "having only two functions, that of raising food "and that of consuming it."* Many a reader may be startled to learn such truths. They are exposed to every Englishman in India, and will every day receive some new and strong corroboration.

Before I enter upon a consideration of the extent to which the people of India may be permitted by their masters to become prosperous and civilized, and of the means by which that object may be attained, I shall review the theories that have met with most attention; since they will act as the safest guides to us in devising new plans for our future progress. I shall commence with that scheme which is calculated to reduce the natives of India to mental ignorance, "to animals having just two functions, that of raising food, and that of consuming it;" and, as the doctrines it inculcates have been the most extensively adopted, and are still in fashion, I shall be excused for a little prolixity, and some repetitions that can with difficulty be avoided, when fully exposing the fallacy of a scheme, that is in itself loosely put together in many of its parts. The names of the lawgivers who broached and acted upon this plan are, Sir Thomas Munro, Lord William Bentinck, Mr. Thackeray, Mr. Ravenshaw, Mr. Shaw, Mr.

---

* Supplement to Ency. Brit., Article "Colony."

Gahagan, and Mr. Chaplin; all gentlemen of the Civil Service, or Government of Madras, at no distant period.

One of the great and obvious objections to the plan followed by these gentlemen is, that it is erected "on expedients instead of principles."—Were I not, from the known character of Sir Thomas Munro, perfectly assured that his motives originated in the purest desire to benefit his Government, and improve the condition of its subjects; were I not satisfied that this distinguished public servant believed in the justice and humanity of his own theory; I should, as a mere reader of his rules, assert that he must have allowed a narrow policy to contract the scope of his fine understanding; in short that, wilfully neglecting principles, he had attended entirely to expediency. That Sir Thomas Munro firmly believed that India was only to be retained by the British Government through the mental incapacity of its inhabitants; that he believed "knowledge is power," and that such power if acquired by the natives of India, would be exercised to eradicate the British sovereignty, and that therefore they ought not to be allowed to acquire it; cannot, I imagine, be disputed by his warmest advocates. But, that he also imagined he was spreading, by the means pursued to attain these primary objects, Arcadian bliss and content among the poorest classes of the community, is equally incontestible.

As the design of these pages is to expose and to inculcate truth, I shall be pardoned for quoting at length the approved sentiments of well informed and learned men, in their own words, instead of re-casting them in language of my own, in token of my concurrence or disapproval. Indeed, my object is chiefly to agitate an important question, and to set before the public strong lights from the works of more able politicians than myself.

In the 5th paragraph of Sir Thomas Munro's despatch to Mr. Petrie, dated the 26th of August, 1805, after mentioning that the great drawback on large estates is the subdivision of property according to Hindoo law, he adds; "Great "estates, though they may be created, cannot "be of long duration in any province in India:" and in the 7th paragraph he says, "There is not "the same necessity in this country as in Europe "for a body of great or rich landlords; and even "if such a body could be raised up, it would "probably in the end be productive of more "harm than good; because great landholders "would in time become impatient of the do-"minion of a foreign nation, and their wealth "and the smallness of their numbers would "enable them to form combinations, which the "class of cultivators have neither the means nor "the wish of attempting." Although the letter which contains these observations was written to establish another in disparagement of Lord Cornwallis's Zemindary plan, they exhibit the views of policy entertained by their author, and are a key to the system which he himself proposed. The inconsistency of the two opinions that "*great estates* could not, from subdivision, "be of long duration;" and, "that their pos-"sessors would *in time*, from the *smallness* of "their numbers, and their wealth, become for-midable to the Government," is very striking; but what I wish to draw attention to is the proposition, that there exists not the *necessity* in this country, as in Europe, for a body of great landlords. The fallacy broached and palmed upon us, under the term "*necessity*," is obvious upon a moment's reflection. If the reader will clothe the argument in these words, its true colour and tendency will be seen: "In "Europe there exists a body of great landlords "who enjoy much happiness from possessing "the good things of this life; who contribute "extensively to the happiness of myriads of "others by employing them in the production "of articles of comfort and luxury, and by "calling forth among them science and talent of "every kind; who assist the King in aggran-

"dizing their nation by the exertion of their "wisdom and influence in the country; and "Europe and Europeans deserve the enjoyment "of this state of things; in fact, *it is necessary* "for Europe, and Europeans, that this state of "things should exist; but there is *no necessity* "that the natives of India should be similarly "circumstanced. There is *no necessity* for an en-"lightened European nation to civilize its tawny "subjects, or to allow them to acquire the things "most highly prized by that nation itself, and "by all other races of men." It will hardly be doubted that Sir Thomas Munro must have been under the influence of fear for the loss of India to Britain, when he proposed to legislate for it on such expedients. Had he forgotten that there was an imperative *necessity* that Government should perform its duty to all its subjects, whether white or black, whether near to London or ten thousand miles distant from it? How could he assert that, *if there was a duty*, a necessity *could* exist for swerving from its performance? I will maintain that *if it was a duty* of Government to make great landholders, *a necessity did exist* for their creation. I will maintain that that reasoning is fallacious which leads to the conclusion, that there is *no necessity* for one race of men being rendered as prosperous as another race of men; or that a Government, the very instrument which should discover, introduce, and uphold, whatever is most conducive to the prosperity and happiness of those for whose sake it is called into existence, can maintain such an argument consistently with any known principles of governing, or with its own vitality. "Great landed "property in possession," says Sir Thomas Munro, "occasions turbulence and insubordi-"nation in the holder." This necessary effect of simply holding land must be deemed a chimera of Sir Thomas's, who no doubt added, in his imagination, to the possession of land the possession of baronial power over vassals, and the knowledge of the true ground of the existence of any government at all. "The ten-"dency of the Indian system of Castes and "laws of inheritance," says again Sir Thomas in the letter to which I have above adverted, "al-"ways has been, and must be to keep land "divided into small portions among the Ryots, "and to make the same person labourer, farmer, "and landlord. Why then attempt to subvert an "ancient system, which places the great body of "the Ryots above want, renders them industrious, "frugal, and comfortable, and preserves the sim-"plicity of their manners, and their respect for "public authority?" "There is no people on "earth among whom there is greater subordina-"tion than among the Hindoos, who never saw

" proprietary Zemindars until they were created " by the Company's Government." The whole tenor, in short, of Sir Thomas's writings is to show that he believed it to be the best policy—maintaining, as he did, the proposition that Government was the owner of the soil, and could do with it what it pleased—to keep the people down, if I may so express myself; and that he hailed those circumstances in their laws and condition which might enable us to do so without appearing to innovate. The true philanthropist would have said: " Why not attempt to supersede a " system by which the great body of the people " have been consigned to indigence for many " ages, especially as Government is the owner of " the land, and may dispose of it to whom, and " on what terms it pleases ? "

That Sir Thomas Munro might have overcome the obstacle of Hindoo law and Caste custom, in respect to the subdivision of landed property is not even problematical. The circumstances of the people and of the land leave this fact unquestionable. They were merely tenants at will, shifting from field to field, (I adopt Sir Thomas's assertions, and am not writing from my own knowledge,) and the land belonged to Government. He had an opportunity, which I fear will hardly be found in any other part of India, of easily bettering the condition of a people, every one of whose own great rulers we had displaced, and to whom we had entirely and permanently blocked up every avenue to advancement. We had annihilated Polygars, Zemindars, and others, the gentry of the community. Our armies and civil offices present not a post worthy of the ambition of any but men in utter want; yet it is by the bravery and intelligence of those natives who fill these low stations, in both departments, that we govern the country: and may not that bravery and that intelligence, if any should finally remain, one day penetrate the veil of security in which we have, at present, wrapped ourselves, and produce a revolution that will be bloody and tremendous, in proportion to the ignorance of the mass of those who will be led to execute it?

I shall now proceed to take into consideration the dogmas of Sir Thomas Munro's supporters. They, like others in similar cases, go further than their master, and wear his theory thread-bare; so that if, from his prudence in not dwelling too much on doubtful points, it may be possible to misunderstand the scope of his maxims, by their forwardness and zeal we distinctly ascertain them. Among his scholars, the sentiments of Mr. Thackeray, advocated by Lord William Bentinck, first demand notice.

His Lordship on the 29th of April, 1806, says in a minute which he was submitting to his government, "I have the honour to lay before "the Board, a paper drawn out by Mr. W. "Thackeray under *my own inspection.*"

In reference to the Zemindary system, the very first proposition of Mr. Thackeray's is, "The power of the Government will be cur-"tailed," and his reasoning proceeds thus, "In "all countries it may be good to limit the power "of the prince, but *here* the Government must "keep as much power as is consistent with "private rights in its own hands." It will scarcely be doubted that no government ever retains less power in its own hands than is consistent with private rights, how much more soever it may seize and maintain; nor will any one dispute that what is good in "*all*" countries, ought certainly to be good "*here*;" for I can affirm that the inhabitants of India are men, and that they have an appetite for, and enjoy, the good things of this life, with as much relish as other men, when they are fortunate enough to procure them. The conclusion drawn by Mr. Thackeray from these pithy premises will not, I hope, induce any reader to infer that Mr. Thackeray was writing nonsense. It is this: "It will *therefore* be right to limit the "demand from the land, but still to keep up as "much communication with the people as possible."—"The waste (the waste land) is the "grand means of improving the people; turning "the Peon into the husbandman"—in Mr. Mill's words, "increasing every year the proportion of "the population which you employ in raising "food, and diminishing every year the population employed in every thing else, until "things arrive at that pass, that men would "have food, but they would have nothing else." "Would it not be better," say Lord William Bentinck and Mr. Thackeray, "that *all* these "people should *look up to the Sircar*, and inasmuch as regards the support of our authority, "that the influence, information, and assistance, "which these people can afford, should be at "the service of Government?" "The *first* "thing," say they again, "is to *govern* the "country; *then* to govern it *well*." These are the maxims of the legislators whose systems have been approved for India. Adjusted to their own systems to support them, or opposed to those of others to discredit them, their weakness escapes the detection of the superficial examiner; but can the king or his ministers for a moment tolerate the assertion, in respect to any class of his Majesty's subjects, that the good government of them is a secondary consideration? Will it be asserted that the rights by conquest of a government abolish the rights of a people to be well governed, except as a secondary consideration? and that they ought to subject them to any kind of tyranny, provided that tyranny be ours? It is the certainty that we wish to evade, and actually to trample on, the rights of our subjects, that incites us to degrade them in the scale of human beings: and is the happiness that might be diffused among millions, is the gratitude of an enlightened people, to be abandoned, because a few alarmists terrify us from the performance of our duty? I rely, and the poor Hindoo relies on the justice of his Majesty's Government to prevent so overwhelming and extensive a calamity. The same power and intelligence by which India was subdued will maintain supremacy over it for generations; and when its sceptre shall be wrested, as it no doubt one day will be, from the hands of the British sovereigns, let them enjoy the gratification of reflecting on the wisdom and justice of their ancestors, in having laid the foundation of such institutions as prepared for its transfer to the hands of an enlightened native prince, or for the establishment of the free constitution of a civilized nation, which will carry on and complete the structure thus commenced.

Mr. Thackeray goes on to deprecate the

Zemindary plan, and to uphold the Ryotwarie, or Sir Thomas Munro's plan, in these terms:— "It is said, that the Zemindar is the proprietor, "the Ryot the occupant; but how undefined are "their repective rights! Nobody has clearly "defined them yet." This passage was written in proof of Mr. Thackeray's general objection, that "the division of the proprietary right of "the Zemindars and occupant right of the "Ryots is bad."—Will the reader believe, however, that what is shown to be good for the Government, could possess an inherent property of evil for an individual standing in its place in a limited sphere? Yet, in the elucidation of his ninth argument Mr. Thackeray observes, "It "may be said that the revenue will *not* be "secure under a Ryotwaur settlement; how-"ever, if the Ryots be put on such a foot-"ing that their lands are saleable, and that "they ought to pay *whether they cultivate or no*, "the *revenue will be secure*, and their lands will "be the security:—no other variations will arise, "but from waste being brought into cultivation. "It is a practice to give up their old lands and "take waste; because the cultivation of waste "under a cowle, is often more favorable to the "Ryot than the cultivation of their own land on "the full rent: but, as the Ryot will be obliged "to pay his rent, whether he cultivates or no, he

" never will take waste till he can afford to " cultivate both the old land and the waste." " And why should not the Zemindar's revenue " *be secure,* if the Ryots were put on such a " footing that their lands are saleable, and that " they ought to pay whether they cultivate or " no? Why should it not be as secure to a " Zemindar as to Government?" Such is the reasoning of Mr. Thackeray—he first lays down his dictum, that a division of two distinct rights is bad; and instead of showing us why, he tells us that the reason of their separation being bad is, that nobody—not even himself—understands them! He afterwards proves, but without perceiving it, that the Zemindar could collect his revenue as easily at least as Government!

" It is very proper," says the legislating Mr. Thackeray, in his paper of the 4th of August, 1807, " that in England a good share of the " produce of the earth should be appropriated " to the support of certain families in affluence, " to produce senators, sages, and heroes, for the " service and defence of the state; or in other " words, that great part of the rent should go to " an opulent nobility and gentry, who are to " serve their country in Parliament, in the army " and navy, in the departments of science, and in " the liberal professions. The leisure, independ- " ence, and high ideas, which the enjoyment of "this rent affords, have enabled them to raise "Britain to the pinnacle of glory. Long may "they enjoy it! but in India, that haughty "spirit, independence, and deep thought, which "the possession of great wealth sometimes gives, "*ought* to be suppressed. *They are directly* "*adverse to our power and interest.* The *nature* "of things, the past experience of *all* Govern-"ments, render it *unnecessary* to enlarge on this "subject. *We* do not want generals, statesmen, "legislators; *we want industrious husbandmen.*" Mr. Thackeray has forgotten to state what the *natives* want, and do not want. "The nature "of things" does not render it necessary or expedient that any consideration should be given to *their* wants. After thus showing, however, what *we* want and, I may be allowed to say, what the natives of India *do not* want; that we want all the good things of this life, while the natives of India do not want them, and only want to be industrious husbandmen; the reader may, perhaps, smile at the following glowing description of the quantity of real comfort and happiness which we leave them, after taking so abundant a portion of the goodly loaves and fishes to ourselves. "It is *our duty* to consider "the happiness of the mild, industrious race "which Providence has placed under the British "Government, *before* revenue, or any other "objects. The domestic happiness, *independence*, "and pleasure, of a country life, which the dis-"tribution of landed property *alone* can confer "on the multitude, make this far superior to any "system. It may be considered an Utopia *by* "*some;* however, *I* think that Government *can*, "and ought, to extend this happy system to "these provinces."

Mr. Thackeray is far from thinking, however, that the Hindoos have no talent for acquiring property, or for enjoying themselves with it after its acquisition. He states that "the people of "the towns, in which property is secured by "Courts of Justice, take as much pains, run as "great risks, and succeed as well, as any people "in the world in acquiring property," and that, "those sages, whose works are read in our "schools, whose books in a great measure form "the minds of our statesmen, learned their wis-"dom from India and Egypt." "The natives," continues this sage, "have clear heads, powers "of application, and perseverance, in a greater "degree than Europeans relaxed in India;" and this is, no doubt, a convenient reason enough for reducing to, and keeping the people in, poverty and ignorance, that we may not be liable to have our heavy repose interrupted by an actively conducted rebellion. The legislating philanthropist then reviews the machine of

Government. " Our Government is so just, so " strong, so wise, in comparison to Native " Governments, that almost under any system, " the country will, *in a certain degree,* prosper :" —" A people so industrious will thrive in spite " even of a bad system, just as a stout child " grows and becomes a sturdy youth in the " midst of rags and poverty. Under the " harshest tyranny, the Ryots seem never to " have relinquished the labours of husbandry; " they consider themselves *born to plough,* and " they labour in their vocation until their " strength fails. The people in the Ceded Dis- " tricts continued to cultivate, though exposed " not only to the arbitrary exactions of their " own Government, but also of banditti. Men " might be seen holding the plough with black " stumps of fingers burnt off by the officers of " their own Government." In short, the Hindoos, Mr. Thackeray would make us believe, have an inextinguishable propensity to be ploughmen, and are so much under the influence of heated imaginations about the Utopian pleasures of a country life and domestic happiness, that their deeply implanted taste for these rural enjoyments is not to be reached and eradicated even by actual cautery! With all deference to Mr. Thackeray, I should say that the Hindoos *were born to live,* and that, finding their only chance of effecting this object was *to plough* the land, they submitted to the lesser evil of torture rather than of death by starvation.

That Lord William Bentinck concurred in most of the views of Sir Thomas Munro, Mr. Thackeray, and others, their supporters, in as far as the discussion had come before him, is undoubted; yet that distinguished statesman disclaims a perfect conviction of their truth and propriety; and it is but justice to him to record in his own words what he says on this point:—" I wish," says his lordship, " to have the opportunity of " ascertaining upon the spot the truth of my " own ideas and the reality of the objections " suggested by others. It is with this view, and " for the purpose of provoking discussion, that " the paper now presented (Mr. Thackeray's " Memoir) has been drawn up." He adds, " I " have no object in view but truth and the pub- " lic good. My imagination and judgment may be " deceived; but I fancy, and am fully persuaded, " that the hapiness of millions depends upon the " decision of this question." *

From what I have just stated, the reader will perhaps be inclined to think that the Ryotwaur, or individual settlement, of Sir Thomas Munro, was bottomed on a policy, and supported by

---

* Appendix to the 5th Report, pages 919 and 920.

arguments, disgraceful to the British Government. Yet, the apparent simplicity, the Arcadian pretensions, of the plan, have blinded the judgment of able statesmen, who, satisfied with the grand advantage which it presented of reducing the chances of rebellions, too readily coincided in a scheme which boasted of ensuring happiness to millions of human beings. They little dreamed that the bliss which they were conferring was that of mere animal existence; that they were consigning nations of individuals to the occupation of consuming in rags poor food, raised with hard labour and frequent uncertainty. And this is the present condition of almost the whole of the British subjects under the Madras Presidency, and is rapidly becoming that of the recent conquests from the Mahrattas under Bombay.

But the Ryotwaur system, although our collectors never burn the husbandman's fingers, is not so very mild and Utopian in its operation as its authors perhaps wished it to be, or at least would lead us to believe. Mr. Thackeray, in discussing the security of the Government revenue under its adoption, remarks :—" If any " doubt should still remain, respecting the " security of the land-tax, a Zunjeer-Żamin, or " several and joint security, may be entered into " with the Ryots of villages, who may be made " responsible for each other, villages for villages, "pergunnas for pergunnas. This system is "termed unjust, and may be thought too complicated for permanency. Respecting the "justice of it, it is ABSOLUTELY NECESSARY to "establish it, in order that the Ryots may have "the enjoyment of the benefits proposed to be "given to them. It is done for *their* sake, and "they *ought* not to complain, nor would they "*when they understood it.* It is no hardship to "make a man give security and let him out of "prison." (Mr. Thackeray's position really and truly is to make a man give security *for any other man,* and then let him out of prison.) "In "respect to *the policy* of the Zunjeer-Zamin, it "makes the bulk of the people interested in the "skill, exertion, and economy, of each individual. "They will assist him to prevent his failing, and "to avoid being called on to fulfil their security. "If he does fail, they take care that there are no "tricks, that his property be discovered and sold "to the best advantage, and they will generally "prevent the necessity of an assessment to make "up his deficiency. If, however, he has no pro-"perty, and their ingenuity can discover nothing, "and hit on no means of settling the demand "without, an assessment is laid on fairly, so "that there are no tricks and no unequal im-"position."

It is for the sake and benefit of the people

that Government takes good care not to lose its amount of revenue by any kind of law! The Ryots were to invent an ingenious method of producing money from a person without property! All this was absolutely necessary, not for the Government interests;—no, but "in "order that the Ryots may have the enjoyment "of the benefits proposed to be given to them." No wonder, indeed, that they were dull enough not to understand such a theory and practice; a theory that presented a gross blunder, wilfully adopted, or committed through ignorance of local usage; a practice which fully proved our charity to begin at home. From one end of India to the other, the Government, before our conquest, never settled with the Ryots individually, not even in years when it surveyed the lands of individuals or villages. If exceptions to this practice are adducible, they are so few that they amount to no tangible qualification of the general usage described.

Sir Thomas Munro himself says—"But as "few Amildaurs, who have not before been in "the Company's service have ever seen a Kulwaur (that is, the Ryotwaur or individual) "settlement, people are sent from the Kutcherry "to carry it into execution." Although therefore it is literally true that the annual Ryotwaur settlement must be made by "somebody," it does not follow that it could be made by *any body*, without an innovation perhaps in the usages of the people ; and very likely without an infringement of the rights of some one or all of the Ryots. It does not follow for instance that, because the Patail and villagers settled the division of the assessment among themselves from time immemorial, other Government agents could, without innovating, abrogate that usage and make the distribution themselves. Sir Thomas Munro misled Government and deceived himself, when he stated and imagined that Amildaurs, or collectors, in former times ever took, as he and his officers did, the duty of distributing the assessment by individuals, into their own hands. Their having done so was an innovation, and its awkwardness in respect to the security of the revenue was fully developed, in the absolute necessity which the innovators were under of adopting the principle of making each man responsible for the failure of others; though in the same breath, they assured the people that they were responsible only as individuals for the extent of their own cultivation. The old custom of the country was this—The Patail let those lands of the village not occupied by Mirassadaurs, or by hereditary tenants, as he best could, to assist in relieving himself and those permanent occupants in discharging the fixed rent or assessment payable by him and those, as a body corporate, for all the lands of the village. This fixed rent was ascertained by a measurement or appraisement of the lands, and in most provinces was denominated Tunkha, or where a later appraisement had been made, Kamil, or Kumaul. In other provinces the crops were annually inspected by the officers of Government, and the amount payable by the body corporate of the village for the year was determined upon fixed principles of computation; yet, in such cases, the aggregate for the year bore reference to the general excellence of the crops. The sum total for the year being known, the village corporation assembled in the village hall, or under a tree; and a distribution of the burden was made according to their respective obligations as land-owners, or hereditary occupants; and, with reference, in particular instances, to the cultivation of the year, and the amount receivable, by special agreement, from tenants at will, for the occupation of portions of waste land. The invention and imposition by tyrannic governments of extra cesses, only prove the existence of a fixed village-rent previously to their exaction; and the exception proves the rule.

That Mr. Thackeray knew that the lands of villages were possessed as a joint stock, by the

Ryots inhabiting each, is learnt from his Report on the Zemnes and assessment of Canara and Malabar, dated 4th of August, 1807, where he says—" The great difference between the lands " in these two provinces, and those *in all other* " provinces is, that here it is vested in in- " dividuals;—*there in communities.* The vil- " lages above the Ghauts are like corporations, " communities, municipalities, republics, *who are* " *proprietors of the whole lands of the villages;* " at least they and the Sircar share the qualities " of property between them. They have cleared " and cultivated the village lands, *time out of* " *mind,* and there is none but the Sircar who can " claim any share in the property from them."

We are told, nevertheless, by the advocates of this system, that no man's property was disturbed by it. It was too Utopian. Some of them allow that hereditary occupants of the land existed; village or joint proprietorship is admitted by others: while some deny the existence of hereditary occupancy, or joint property, in all provinces excepting Arcot, Canara and Malabar. Sir Thomas Munro's own allegations are, " All " land is supposed to revert to Government at " the end of every year, to be distributed as it " may think proper; and land is accordingly " sometimes taken from one Ryot and given to " another who is willing to pay a higher rent.

" In the Ceded Districts and throughout the " Deccan, the Ryot has little or no property in the " land, he has no possessory right, he does not " even claim it." Yet, in the very same letter (dated 15th August, 1807) where Sir Thomas advances these observations, he proposes a *joint responsibility*, and the imposition of 10 per cent. *upon the rent of every Ryot;* not 10 per cent. of the defalcation, as some have imagined, to reimburse Government for the failure of other Ryots. It may not however be out of place to show the inconsistency of Sir Thomas Munro's opinion on this subject:—" The tendency of the Indian " system of Castes always has been and must " be to keep the land divided among the Ryots, " and to make the same person labourer, farmer, " and *landlord.* Why then attempt to subvert " an ancient system ?" &c. Here Sir Thomas alleges that the land belonged to individuals; before, that it was exclusively the property of the Sircar: and the question is suggested—If the ancient system we are called upon *not to subvert*, contemplated the Ryot as landlord, how did it come to pass that " the land reverted to Govern- " ment at the end of every year ?" And we are left to conjecture which state of the people was considered by Sir Thomas Munro, as the ancient one. Whether Sir Thomas Munro, when he broached his Ryotwarry system, was aware of the joint village responsibility, I have not discovered from his writings; but he could not have advanced very far in the practice of his plan without seeing it staring him in the face. The result was a clumsy patching together of the two distinct obligations of a joint and several responsibility, under the title of an individual settlement. It is not surprising that the Ryots could not understand how they were at once to be individually and jointly responsible, when the source of indemnification, the waste land, was withdrawn from their controul. The fact is, the revenues of Government were found to be in jeopardy through the Ryotwarry innovation, and resort was had to the ancient custom of the country, after the vital principle of its existence, the waste land, had been exhausted. If the advocates of the system shall say that I have attributed this invention to an erroneous origin, they must then be content to admit that Sir Thomas Munro was guilty of a greater blunder, than I think can be laid to his charge—the establishment of an *unknown and unprecedented usage,*—an innovation of the most unpalatable kind, as he did not, at the same time, transfer the waste lands to the Ryots, as bodies corporate, to enable them to indemnify themselves by foresight and additional industry for the additional impost; but left them to discover by *ingenuity* latent resources, or to *hit upon* some curious expedient to relieve themselves from an unjust burden. Even supposing the Ryots had more intelligence than they possess, and could understand that, if they did not pay to Government an amount sufficient for its expenses in defending them from foreign invasion and domestic plunder, they would be liable to those evils; still, they might with justice have required, that the mercantile classes of the community, and the native and English gentlemen, who had more property at stake than they, should be taxed in the deficient quota, rather than that they should themselves be deprived of their last farthing, on account of the carelessness or thriftlessness of other men, with whose agricultural affairs they had, on the other principles of the Ryotwarry settlement, no more necessary connexion than the richest individual of the community had. But then comes the question—Was such or such a sum proved to be necessary for the protection of the people from foreign aggression and internal robbers? This is a point so intimately blended with what is necessary for *our own* domestic stability *as a Government*, that it would be difficult to determine with any degree of precision how much money is required for the wants of the State, in affording adequate protection, and administering their laws to the people; and how much for the maintenance of our own political supremacy. The public here does not, as in England, assess itself on a just cause being shown for the expenditure. Had those who pay the taxes here the privilege of scrutinizing our accounts, what a reduction should we see in the expenditure for the equipment of the military, and for all the grades of military officers; in short, in all those circumstances of our power which aid in supporting *our* supremacy? What a reduction in the salaries of judges and collectors! As it is, *we* are the only judges of the taxation as well as of the expenditure. We have even looked forward to a surplus revenue being remitted to Britain. Yet Bengal says to Bombay—" You " must pay your own expenses." This reasoning, the Hindoo would tell us, is wrong, in both instances. No surplus revenue, he would argue, should ever be sent to Britain: and as Bombay is an integral portion of the British Empire, and Bengal subsists by the aid of Bombay, and *vice versa,* the factitious charges of our political supremacy ought to be equally borne by the peasants of both countries. The Hindoos would further say of Sir Thomas Munro's assertion—" Land-rent is to the Indian what the " Excise and Customs are to the English revenue;" the sooner land-rent is the least source of revenue by direct taxation, the sooner will India be rich, like England, by indirect taxation. But Mr. Thackeray declares that what we do is "for the sake of the natives," in order that they may enjoy "the benefits" he had devised for them; and that "they ought not "to complain, nor would they when they under-"stood it." I confess I think the better "they "understood it" the more loud would be their complaints; and perhaps Mr. Thackeray had some smothered belief of this kind himself, since his scheme obviously is, to reduce them to, and keep them in, utter ignorance, so as to deprive them of the power of judging for themselves.

But to review the Ryotwaur system effectually, it will be proper to consider it on all the grounds assumed both by its advocates and its opponents, when discussing its merits as a fiscal arrangement; and this will lead me to remark on its effects, or probable results, and on the various actual or assumed conditions of the people, where it has been or may yet be introduced. I may class these conditions of the agriculturists under three heads:—The first, in which the Ryot was a landowner, or possessed an hereditary title of occupying land:—the second, in which the Ryot was a tenant at will, working on the land of Government:—the third, in which, being either landlord or tenant at will, he was responsible to Government for the failures of other Ryots, with whom he was associated in a joint responsibility for the full discharge of the Government dues of the village, or body corporate.

The disputants respecting Ryotwaur settlements have either wilfully, or unwittingly, misunderstood and mixed up two plans, running, it is true, into each other in many particulars, but different, in as far as the one contemplated a precise ascertainment of the rent of fields; whereas the other did not effect this object, and left the assessment higher than the country could bear. The latter plan was the first acted upon. It was that adopted by Colonel Read, and the defence of it was abandoned both by himself and Colonel Munro, as a permanent system of management. The former gentleman, in his letter to his assistants, dated the 12th April, 1798, says, "Patails and "other farmers can determine the actual value "of the land with tolerable exactness, but "they never will do that for us, or report the "occupancy of it; all that is now left to be "done with fidelity. Our next dependence is "on our Mootesiddies; but, self-interested, they "will either favour the Ryots or cheat the Sircar; "or, pretending zeal for the service, impose

" on both." Colonel Munro saw the same defects and many more. There was no certain ground for acquiring a knowledge of the truth. " The Aumildaur," says Sir Thomas, in his letter to his assistants, dated the 25th of August, 1802, " sensible of the danger of an extra assessment, " seldom ventures upon it, but usually prefers " the safer mode of fabricating stories of loss " of crops, and other accidents, and of the " inability of the inhabitants to discharge the " balances." And so completely was the collector destitute of the means of applying a suitable check to these corrupt practices of his own agents, that Sir Thomas was driven to defend this weak point of system by a rule-of-three contrivance in judgment, that may amuse the reader. " When such excuses are " received, *it ought invariably to be concluded,* " unless the facts are very fully established, " that there is *something* wrong in his conduct, " and his removal from office ought to follow " without delay:" and this was the only substantial check to prevent the Ryot from being plundered by Government agents, the collector from being hoodwinked, and the resources of the state from being alienated. Sir Thomas further tells us, " The Patails and Curnums, " when they know that the Aumildaur diverts " a part of the public revenue to his own "emolument, *always* follow his example, and "thereby augment the outstanding balance. "They frequently go further," &c. It will hardly be disputed, from such a description, that the collector was at the mercy of his own native establishment; and that, instead of being a check over them, he, by confirming with his own seal and signature all their acts during the settlement, shut out every chance of the Ryots' condition being made known to him. "Whenever," says Sir Thomas Munro, in his letter dated the 30th of September, 1802, "the "individual settlement of a District is com- "pleted, pottahs for every Ryot paying rent to "Government, should be made out by the "Curnums and transmitted to the Kutcherry, "*to be signed by you*, after having been com- "pared,"—and *with what* were they to be compared? With the settlement effected by "those who could best conduct it," by the collector's native establishment! and *by whom* were they compared? by the same establishment; for the collector neither could, nor ever did, himself compare them. The chain was thus completed by which the collector confirmed whatever might be dishonest in his establishment, and the Ryot was debarred complaint; for the authority to whom he could complain was that which had confirmed the oppression. And even if, not attending to the dissuasions of interested Aumildaurs and Patails, the Ryot did muster up courage to lodge a complaint, the collector (unless it was the just Sir Thomas Munro himself) would, in general, rather feel irritation against the petitioner, than an inclination to repeal his own act. But, as Colonel Munro abandoned the support of this system, excepting under new restrictions and checks, he is only of course accountable for the effects of it under the novel circumstances. The *new* Ryotwarry plan was as much an assessment by fields as by Ryots: the objects it was projected to attain by its introduction were—to equalize the assessment of land, by surveying and rating it according to its quality and other data: to make the assessment low enough to induce the Ryots to occupy certain portions of land permanently and hereditarily: and to enable Government to conclude, as in the old plan, its annual settlement with each individual renter or proprietor of lands, of one or of more fields.

I now beg leave to direct attention to the applicability of the last mentioned plan to the different conditions of the people to which I have adverted; and also to its effects on these conditions.

If we suppose the Ryots, to whose villages

the new Ryotwarry plan was to be applied, possessed an hereditary title to the lands which they occupied, I see only one objection to its introduction; for with that exception, it would confirm the existing state of things. But the exception is of the first importance. It will at once be perceived that, to equalize the assessment of lands according to their actual condition and fertility, would have been an unjust infringement of the rights of the land-owners. He, whose ancestors, or who himself had spent capital and industry in the improvement of his estate; who had, by his care and exertions, rendered that estate doubly or trebly valuable and productive; would have had his payment to Government doubly or trebly increased, and the value of his estate, if he wished to sell it, much diminished: and he, whose estate remained unimproved, would have had to pay the same as he paid before. Industry would have been punished, and improvidence encouraged. The true landmark of the just and fixed assessment of land, its natural capacity, would have been lost sight of, and probably obliterated, and a fluctuating principle of assessment acknowledged and introduced, bearing reference to the actual condition of the land, and, consequently, in most cases, to the actual circumstances of the individual. It is true, that there was a maximum point in the scheme, but by what justice could it be applied to this tenure? Its adoption would be an encroachment on the value of property, and an infringement of the just expectations and rights of the individuals; for, if it was not, what other end could the re-assessment produce, under its equalizing principles? The great mass of the lands is unimproved: Government derives its greatest revenue from the great mass of the lands: it could not possibly contemplate, therefore, the reduction of the rent of the great mass of the lands to so low a condition as to leave the rent of improved lands, or rather of the most highly improved lands, just what it was. But if it did not equalize downwards, it must have done so upwards, and thus produced the effects that I have stated. It is precisely the great fault of Asiatic taxation, that it never provides for reaching the pocket of the subject by indirect imposts, when the prosperity of the people would warrant its doing so; and that the agricultural class, unable to conceal their improvements, have been a never ceasing object of attack and additional taxation to the short-sighted legislator or the tyrant of the time. We do not therefore find much land highly improved in India; but still there is plenty, moderately increased in value: and it is on the owners of such land that the equalizing principle would act with injustice. It is pretty evident, I think, that Sir Thomas Munro was not aware that the condition of the people was such as I have described it in these provinces, to which he recommended the application of his plan. In fact, in Malabar and Canara, the only two provinces where landlord proprietors were found by him, he neither made, nor, in as far as I am informed, recommended a new assessment; but, on the contrary, he took these countries as the land-mark of his own plan for setting down, in a different condition of the people, migratory Ryots as landed proprietors. We may therefore allow Sir Thomas the credit of seeing the injustice of equalizing the assessments of landlords, according to the actual condition of their estates. In fact, I find but one instance of the advocates of the Ryotwarry plan, having any where declared it to be applicable (I speak of the new plan and assessments) to existing landed proprietors and their estates. This instance* has occurred in that part of the Deccan, conquered from the Peshwa, during the last Mahratta war, where the Ryots have in general an absolute property in the soil, and where the tax on their

* See Note A.

estates, or their share of the village assessment, as members of a body corporate, appears to be even better ascertained, and much more moderate than in Canara and Malabar. The Bombay Government contemplates neither an increase nor a decrease of its resources from this measure, except in the discovery of unduly alienated or concealed lands. But, as the rules for the survey and re-assessment of that country are chiefly founded on Sir Thomas Munro's equalizing data and maximums of rent, and are edited by Mr. Chaplin, one of the great advocates of the Ryotwaur system, it might be inferred that Mr. Chaplin had either mistaken the latitude of the application of Sir Thomas's plan, or, that he has carried it no further than its author calculated it might go. In either case, however, it was necessary to view its application to this condition of the people. My own opinion is, that Sir Thomas would either not have applied it at all, or have done so with as much reservation as his follower has done under the wise guidance of Mr. Elphinstone's government. A survey alone, to discover concealed lands, and to ascertain other particulars, whether respecting land tenures or the extent of land, would be quite unobjectionable: but, I imagine, that the re-assessment of landed estates upon principles of equalization must be deemed unjust; and that therefore the strict Ryotwaur plan is so far inapplicable to this condition of the agriculturists.

The effects on the people of the application of the plan to a country of landlords, would be to reduce them, at once, from a better to a worse condition. They would be placed on a par with tenants at will, both as regards the value of land and competition for the sale of its produce. To a landlord of any substance the new assessment would have still worse consequences—he would lose many of his tenants; "for," as Sir Thomas Munro says, "as there is "every where plenty of good land lying un-"cultivated, which any person may occupy on "paying the Sircar rent, it is evident that no "Ryot will hold land of another, and pay an "addition of five or six per cent upon the "Sircar rent, when he may get land of the "same kind without paying any such increase." That this effect would be produced is not a subject of speculation; for, in countries occupied by landlords where the Ryotwarry system has been introduced, and the waste lands taken from the villagers as a body corporate, to be let out by Government without even a revised assessment, (that is, on the first or old Ryotwarry plan) the passion of collectors to show an increase of cultivation in their returns, "to turn the Peon into the husbandman," has nearly ruined the landed proprietors. Land of the best quality, requiring little labour to bring it under the plough, was let to tenants at will, at low rates, progressively increasing in a series of years to the standard village rate. These cultivators of course easily undersold most of the landlords; and the measure has rendered landed property of little or no value now, in comparison with its value in former times. I speak generally, and also in particular, with reference to our late acquisitions in the Deccan. In these provinces Mirassadaurs have been known to abandon the estates which their families had cultivated for centuries, to migrate to another country or village, in order to receive the favourable Cowles (or progressive leases) in the market, drawn out according to the plans of the Madras Ryotwarry collectors, and of the Deccan commissioner, Mr. Chaplin. There can therefore be but one opinion of the deteriorating effect of the encroachment on the rights of the Mirassadaurs, which the Ryotwaur system, whether the old or the new one, is calculated to produce. It cannot fail to reduce the thriving agriculturist to a level* with those who are in the worst circumstances; for,

* See Note B.

in Sir Thomas's words, there is "plenty of good land lying uncultivated," even in Meerassy villages; and which, under the operation of the Ryotwarry plan, whether with or without a survey, falls into the patronage of the Government, whether it previously belonged or not to the village community.

The second condition of the people to which I have adverted, that the Ryot is not, and that the Government is, the owner of the land, is that which is most generally contemplated by the advocates of the Ryotwarry plan, to be peculiarly suited for its application; and perhaps most of them consider this state to be a *sine qua non* towards its appropriate accomplishment. To me there appears not to be an objection to this application of the system:—and therefore I consider the plan to have been framed originally with reference exclusively to this condition of the people. It was surely applicable to it without any breach of faith or justice, and was calculated to improve, on the whole, the circumstances of the Ryots, to a certain but a truly limited extent.

In this case we are to consider that "the "land reverts to Government at the end of "every year;" and "that the Ryot is always "ready to relinquish his land, and to take some "other which he supposes to be more lightly "assessed." The object of the plan was to reverse these circumstances, in as far as the Ryot was concerned; to make the land his, and to fix him down to a particular spot. The means were, the survey and assessment of the land by fields, or small patches; and to the Ryot a perfect freedom of selection and change. Now, to render this scheme effective, it will be evident that there must be the nicest practical discrimination of the productive powers of fields applied to their assessment; and that as much, if not more, must depend upon the precisely proportionate value of each field being determined, as upon the low scale of the assessment of all the fields, to induce the Ryots not to change them. Persons so poor and so unsettled as these Ryots are described to be would not much appreciate the proprietary right intended to be conferred upon them. They would look to the present, and would immediately abandon a field which they had cultivated, to obtain another "which they should suppose "was more lightly assessed." The same nice discrimination would be requisite with respect to granting Cowles for waste lands. If these were too lightly assessed by progressive increases, or if the term of years was too long, then the capital, (small as it may be) and the industry of the country, would be applied to them, and the old lands would be deserted. For this system, therefore, in such a condition of the people, a sufficiently low rent to allow of the property becoming private, and the most precise ascertainment of the relative value, not only of the fields or patches of every village, but of the fields over whole provinces, are the requisite data for success. Montesquieu remarks on the feasibility of such an operation, " In forming a register of the different " classes of landed property, it is very difficult " to ascertain the several differences; *and still* " *more so, to find people who have no interest in* " *mistaking them.* This creates two kinds of " injustice, that which is in the officer of Go- " vernment, and that which is in the thing itself. " But if, on the whole, the tax be not excessive, " if it still leaves plenty to the people, these " particular inequalities are of no moment. If " on the contrary, nothing is left to the people, " but what is precisely necessary for their exist- " ence, the least disproportion will be of the " greatest importance."* I leave it to the advocates of the new assessments to prove that they have in one instance succeeded, in one village only, either to their own satisfaction or

---

* Montesquieu's Spirit of Laws, Book xii. Chap. 7.

that of landowners (of a previous formation) in fixing the assessment of fields in an unexceptionable manner.

But I shall suppose that a perfect assessment is attainable, and has been attained; and that the Ryot who has taken one or more fields feels no inducement whatever to change to other fields. The effect would be that he would become a Mirassadaur of that or those fields. But it is evident that he could never extend his agricultural industry to other fields, until he had reared a progeny who would labour for him; for, as Sir Thomas Munro says, "he would unite in "his own person the characters of farmer, la-"bourer, and landlord." He could not, therefore, occupy more land than he could himself plough and sow. Even if he realized a considerable surplus he could have no under-tenant, "for," says Sir Thomas Munro, "as there is "every where plenty of good land lying uncul-"tivated, which any person may occupy on "paying the Sircar rent, it is evident that no "Ryot will hold land of another and pay an "addition of five or six per cent upon the "Sircar rent, when he may get land of the same "kind, without paying any such increase." I have said a *considerable* surplus, although Sir Thomas Munro contemplates only a small surplus, because it is obvious that the under-tenant would prefer acquiring for himself the whole of this same surplus, "from land of the same kind," whatever it might amount to, rather than be deprived of it; and that he could obtain the *whole* surplus Sir Thomas admits. With but few exceptions, therefore, individuals could never acquire more than the property of one or two fields; for, if a man, by the industry of his sons could take more, still, if they did not during their father's life register some of the new fields in their own names, they certainly would do so after his death. The Hindoo law of succession produces this effect; but this system does the same; for, where the sons can always obtain new land as good as their father's, and upon equal terms of rent and inheritance, it will be a matter of indifference whether they continue to occupy their father's fields by subdividing them among them, or whether they take new land equal to their ability to manage, in lieu of, or in addition to, their portions by inheritance.

As we have supposed the scale of the Government rent to be moderate, we must also conclude that, *if the Ryot were thrifty*, he might, at the end of a considerable period, amass as much money as would enable him to dig a well, or to construct a conduit to convey water to his land from some neighbouring stream. He would thus enhance the value of his estate above that of other estates, so far as the ratio of the maximum rate of rent was less than that of his greater profits. But, in most instances, or rather in all instances, in which the improvement was not much greater than that described, the rate of rent, according to the scheme, nearly kept pace with the increased means of paying it. Allowing, however, that the maximum rate was more favourable to the Ryot, the increased value of the estate which I have stated would be the summit of the improvement; and would furnish the greatest extent of means that one individual was capable of commanding as the result of his industry; for no sooner should the owner of such an estate die, than his sons would, according to the law of partition and that of the Ryotwaur system, be obliged to divide it; and, where there were several sons, each individual would be thrown back, in nine cases out of ten, to as low a state of indigence as his father when he first commenced his farm. Under this system, therefore, there would be no considerable improvement of the people, and but little accession to the resources of Government; for although, in the state of the people I have under review, Government is at liberty to make what terms, and with whom, it should see fit, for the occupation of its land; and it should be, under these circumstances, with strict justice, a part of the plan to raise the rent of irrigated lands, be their produce what it might, to a certain maximum, and further to increase the revenue by the occupation of waste, the old land in cultivation being supposed not to be abandoned for that purpose; still the limit to the improvement of the resources of the State would be very circumscribed, and they would by no means advance so much as they ought to do from the great increase in the population which must ensue. The people would then be kept down, by a never ceasing cause of depression, to a very low state of indigence and ignorance; although on the whole, perhaps, they would be better off than before. We have Sir Thomas Munro's own experience and authority for this assumption in these terms :—" As long as Government " has uncultivated land of a tolerably good " quality to dispose of, *Ryots can have no tenants.*"

Although Sir Thomas Munro himself never anticipated any great improvement of the people from his plan, or expected that it would do more than " place the great body of the Ryots above " want, and render them industrious, frugal, " and comfortable ;" his followers go far beyond him, and venture to surmise, with a laughable gravity, that it was probably too Utopian. They are to be found talking of the plan admitting of such a degree of prosperity, as to allow of the land becoming saleable; just as if, in the first place, it were possible to sell land where it is so plentiful, and so lowly and *equally* assessed that the landlord cannot by possibility, according to the author of the plan, and I may add according to my own experience, obtain an under-tenant; and as if, in the second place, such a state of things as the occupation of even one half of the waste land throughout India generally should ever occur.

But where has the assessment of fields ever been, and where can it ever be so accurately ascertained by Government surveys, as I have imagined? Where can it ever be determined more nearly than just to make the Ryot continually discontented with the field he occupies, or contented with it for no longer than for the term (if indeed so long) of his lease or engagement? "It is the practice to give up their own lands," says Mr. Thackeray, in a paper I have already quoted, "and take waste, because the "cultivation of waste under a Cowle is more "favourable to the Ryot, than the cultivation of "their old land on the full rent; but as the "Ryot will be obliged to pay his rent whether "he cultivates or no, he never will take waste "till he can afford to cultivate both the old land

"and the waste." What then becomes of the boasted *freedom* of the Ryot? Without *forcing* him to settle down to a particular spot, the attractions of waste land, that is of land *unequally** assessed, would instantly unsettle both him and the whole Ryotwaur scheme.

If we throw aside the equalizing principle of the Ryotwaur plan, and at once admit that, in any Government survey and assessment there must be great mistakes, the effect would be precisely what the advocates of the Ryotwaur system wish to make us consider to be attendant on the perfect execution of their plan: that is, wherever the survey failed; wherever it acted just in the very opposite way to what they intended; wherever it produced inconsiderable inequalities of assessment; there, the Ryot would fix himself on the unequally and lowly assessed field, and become its proprietor. But this would not change his power of working more land. He would still be the same circumscribed "farmer, landlord, and labourer," that has been delineated. The same effect would also result from the obliteration of land-marks, by which a man should have more land than he is assessed for; or from any cause, in short, by

---

* See Note C.

which the principles of equality of assessment laid down in the rules of the plan and survey were, to any considerable extent, infringed. Under these circumstances, the lands of a few individuals in each village might become saleable, and the possessors of them might even have under-tenants, contrary to Sir Thomas Munro's own reasoning when he invented the plan. If it had been desirable to allow the existence of landlords who might have under-tenants, it would have been very easy to give away considerable portions of land on favourable and lower terms than certain other lands, to enable the owners of them to hire under-tenants. But this was not by any means what was required at the time Sir Thomas Munro drew out his plan; although it is now adverted to as one of the objects that was to be attained through the future and progressive operation of the system: and we even hear boasts made, where in one or two places some individuals have thriven from a considerable inequality of assessment produced by some of the causes I have mentioned—that is, from a failure of the plan itself—that a landed property has been attained, and that the owner is advancing to be a great landholder, having many under-tenants. It will be obvious to every one, I think, that at first Sir Thomas was far from contemplating such a result from his plan, although he himself latterly would perhaps have been very glad to prove such favourable circumstances to be the result of it. What inferences can be drawn from the following passages applied to each other, and to the reasoning I have brought forward, but that in the survey of the Baramahal country there were ten thousand mistakes, frauds, and erroneous principles; and that, in consequence of the considerable inequalities of the assessment produced by blunders and frauds, some of the land (I do not suppose any one will ever believe that all, or even one fourth of it) has, or ever will, become saleable in Baramahal?* There is indeed no other rational way of accounting for the phenomenon (for such it must be deemed) described by Sir Thomas Munro. In his Minute, dated the 31st of December, 1824, paragraph the 11th, Sir Thomas Munro has said that, "the effect in Baramahal, produced by "the survey assessment, *not from its moderation*, "for it is hardly lighter than that of the native "governments usually is, but from its having "been fixed and so clearly defined as to leave "no uncertainty," has been "*to create saleable* "landed property." "The value and rent of

* See Note D.

" land," says Mr. Thackeray, " fluctuate like the " value of any thing else. But even at present " we cannot so nicely appraise earth, and *if we* " *could*, ten thousand mistakes *must* find their " way into a survey. Frauds *cannot* be pre- " vented, and erroneous principles *are* frequently " adopted." But, although the advocates of the system have, in some places, changed their ground, and would have under-tenants, to satisfy us that the Ryotwaur system can and does produce them; yet they, at the same time, and in the same breath, assert the beauty of its principles *in levying the revenue solely from that class which produces all revenue*,* and which, if it means any thing, we must conclude to mean the actual labourers and ploughmen of the land. Carry this argument a step further, and we should have the ploughing oxen and horses paying a considerable portion of the revenue; brewers' horses taxed for malt liquors, &c. As well, indeed, might I gravely assert that slaves

* There is another watchword or chorus of the advocates of the Ryotwaur system. It is, that the landed proprietors must, and will, always deal with their tenants "as the strong usually deal with the weak:" as if Englishmen had not wit enough to devise checks to oppression; as if they were to shut up their Courts of Justice as soon as landed proprietors were made!

and beasts of burden are not capital, and that free labourers are, as admit that the advocates of the Ryotwaur system have made no blunder in talking of under-tenants being compatible with settling for the Revenue with those who produce it.

As the advocates of the plan inform us, that the Ryot, on becoming the landlord, may sell, bequeath, or give away any portion or the whole of his estate, without interference on the part of Government, they should also have told us what, in such cases, is to become of the land-marks of the fields, and how that portion of the whole estate, which, in some districts, is allowed to be held at a fourth or fifth of the full rent, is to be split up and accounted for. It is my own opinion (shall I not say that I know it to be the fact?) that, the land-marks are every day liable to obliteration, both by accident and design: and that, to retain the registers of fields on the Ryotwaur plan, new surveys would be required at the expiration of short periods.

That this state of the people is adapted therefore for the application of Sir Thomas's Ryotwaurry plan, founded on a re-assessment of the country by fields, is unquestionable. It would occasion no injustice to individuals, while it might, if the Ryots did *voluntarily* settle down to particular fields, tend more to place the people above want, than leaving them to the operation of the system which it was proposed to supersede by its adoption. As a fiscal arrangement, there would be a loss of revenue to Government for the present, to the amount, perhaps, of what it would be requisite to excuse, to induce the Ryots to settle to fields; but there would be little advantage in the end, since the condition and circumstances of the people who pay taxes, although there would be a greater number of them, would be but little improved. There would be no room for them to advance in civilization, or in the employing themselves in other occupations than raising food, each person to a limited and small extent, and consuming it.

Before I enter upon the consideration of the third condition of the people, to which I have adverted, I must beg leave to draw the attention of the reader to the obvious means at Sir Thomas Munro's command, if he believed his own descriptions of the state of the people, for adopting any other plan than that of the Ryotwaur in the Ceded Districts. He declares the land to belong to Government; he describes circumstances to be in existence, the absence of which in Bengal formed the only great bar to the full success of the benevolent plan of Lord Cornwallis; he opposes that, or any plan which should create and maintain a gentry in India.

In a country where he could have done what he pleased with the land, in as far as any other person, by his account, had any claim on it, the only thing he did was to make a bad edition of the tenures of Canara; and yet, when he, or the advocates of his system, find it necessary to defend it, they invariably endeavour to withdraw attention from it, and to fix it on the defects of the Bengal plan; which, however inapplicable in Bengal, was certainly quite applicable in those territories of Madras, where its introduction was resisted by Sir Thomas Munro. Why might not Sir Thomas have given up the land to great or middling, as well as small holders? and, as he could impose any terms as the consequence of the gift, why not have instituted *in respect to it* the law of primogeniture, or imposed great restrictions on the law of division of property? Would not this have been at least as palatable and just as the imposition of 10 per cent. on one Ryot for the failure of another? But such a plan was no part of Sir Thomas Munro's *state policy*. The balance of convenience was to have slaves and a moderate revenue, rather than an intelligent and a wealthy people with a great revenue. It will hardly be disputed that a wealthy capitalist might dig wells and make water-courses, and improve the capabilities of the soil, where the Ryot, who is "labourer, farmer, "and landlord," never could. But I shall discuss this question in some detail in a subsequent part of my subject. "It has been said," remarks Sir Thomas Munro, "that there can be no proper subordination without just gradations of "rank in society;* and that Zemindaurs are "required in Indian society to accomplish this "desirable end. But this opinion is completely "contradicted by experience; for, there is not a "people upon earth among whom there is greater "subordination than among the Hindoos, who "never saw proprietary Zemindaurs until they "were created by the Company's Government." Now, although there never had been Zemindaurs, such as Lord Cornwallis created, yet there had been in most of the provinces of India a local gentry, whose places are now occupied by English gentlemen, well paid, and by native agents of our Government, badly paid; and although this gentry partook of, and were interwoven with, the domestic management of the Government, and were not like independent English gentlemen, yet they formed, to every intent and purpose, gradations of rank in society, and were the natural heads of the people, whom they frequently guarded from

---

* See Note E.

heavy oppressions, although they oppressed them sometimes themselves. But, even if there had been no gentry before, what can we think of the statesman who would not endeavour to engraft them on the stock of society; of him who talks of experience, and says they are neither wanted nor useful, when the most prosperous nations of the earth are distinguished by that characteristic of their society, and the most uncivilized in learning, arts, and sciences, and the poorest in pecuniary resources, are marked by the very reverse? If the Hindoos were in such a state of barbarism, it was Sir Thomas Munro's duty, as a man, as a Briton, and as a legislator for millions, to rescue them from it without delay.

But let us examine and apply the theory of Sir Thomas Munro's plan, with the theories of economists respecting the increase of capital in a nation. I shall quote from the latest and best writers on the subject.

"Without capital, labour would never have "been divided, and men would never have "emerged from barbarism."* The corollary of this proposition evidently is, that the greater the capital, the greater will be the division of labour,

---

* *Edinburgh Review*, No. LXXIX. page 3.

and the less will be the barbarism of those among whom it has been produced. "It is almost "always necessary to provide ourselves with the "results of previous industry, or, in other words, "with capital, and to strengthen our feeble "hands by arming them, if we may so speak, "with the force of all the elements."*

"It is an admitted, and indeed almost a "self-evident principle, that the produce of the "labour of a nation, cannot be increased other-"wise than by *an increase in the number of its "labourers, or by an increase in the skill or pro-"ductive powers of those already existing*. But, "without an increase of capital, it is in most "cases impossible to employ an increased num-"ber of workmen. If the food and clothes "destined for the support of the labourers, and "the tools and machines with which they are "to operate, be all required for the efficient "maintenance and efficient employment of those "now in existence, there can be no additional "demand for others. In such circumstances, the "rate of wages cannot rise; and if the number "of inhabitants increase, they must be worse pro-"vided for. Neither is it possible to augment "the productive powers of the labourer without

---

* *Edinburgh Review*, No. LXXIX. page 3.

"a previous increase of capital, for these powers "can never be materially improved except by "the better education and training of workmen, "by the greater subdivision of their employ-"ments, or by an improvement in the machinery "they are employed to manage. And in all "these cases, an increase of capital is almost "invariably required. It is only by an outlay "of additional capital that the workman can be "better trained, or that the undertaker of any "work can either provide his workmen with "better machinery or make a more proper dis-"tribution of labour among them."*

"Before a man," say with great truth the same writers, "can accumulate, he must live: "and if the sum that remains to him after his "necessary expenses are deducted be but small "and trifling, the probability is, that he will "rather choose to consume it immediately, than "to hoard it up in the expectation that, by the "addition of further savings, it may at some "future and very distant period become the "means of making a small addition to his in-"come. The truth is that the pressure of want "is seldom or never productive of economy. In "a state of indigence, there is neither the power

* *Edinburgh Review*, No. LXXIX. page 3.

" nor the wish to have. Want is the parent of " idleness and dissipation, and not of frugality. " The lower we descend in the scale of society " the less forethought, the less regard to future " and distant consequences, do we find to pre- " vail. The labourer is less prudent than the " little tradesman or shopkeeper, the beggar than " the labourer."*

This description is so truly applicable to the greatest portion of the inhabitants of India, as they are at this day, that a person who has any knowledge of them might suppose that the reviewers had India in their contemplation when they penned it. Another writer assures us that great improvements in the productive powers of labour " arise from the use of those instruments " which form one of the portions of capital. " Great improvements also arise from the " division, including the distribution, of labour." He also says, " A certain immense aggregate of " operations is subservient to the production of " the commodities useful and agreeable to man. " It is of the highest importance that this aggre- " gate should be divided into portions, consist- " ing each of as small a number of operations as " possible, in order that every operation may

---

* *Edinburgh Review*, No. LXXIX. page 5.

"be more quickly and perfectly performed."*
"It thus sufficiently appears," says also Mr. Mill, "that there is a tendency in population to "increase faster than capital. If this be estab- "lished, it is of no consequence to the present "purpose to inquire about the rapidity of in- "crease. How slow soever the increase of popu- "lation, provided that of capital is still slower, "wages will be reduced so low, that a portion of "the population will regularly die of want."†

I shall proceed to consider the effect of the Ryotwaur plan on that condition of the society where the Ryot, possessing, or not possessing, hereditary title to the occupancy of land, was, jointly with other Ryots, as a member of a body corporate, responsible to Government for the failures of other Ryots. And I shall first advert to that condition in which he is a land-owner, or possesses an hereditary title to the occupancy of land.

If all the land-owners of the village held their estates in consideration of the payment of a certain defined share, or portion, of a fixed village assessment, and could, either of themselves or through their Patail, challenge the management

---

* *Mill's Elem. of Pol. Econ.*, pages 10, 11, and 12.

† *Ibid.* page 56.

of other members; or could indemnify themselves for the absence or failure of other members, by joining their stock and labour to plough up the lands of those members, or the waste lands of the village; then, what they were bound to pay or contribute their labour to, as members of the corporation, they might with justice be bound to pay individually, settling themselves with the Government direct: but if the settlement of the Government was made with them for the exact quantity of land in their own estates, and their estates or fields were thus separated from the whole lands, and they themselves from the whole body of land-owners of the village, the tax upon them individually for the failure of their neighbours would be unjust. But the Ryotwaur system has been shown to be an assessment of single fields and estates, and of single individuals for the extent of them, while the waste land, and all that is left uncultivated by proprietors, is claimed* by Government, and let out to any tenant who will occupy it; that tenant paying the rent which he engages to Government, and not to the village as theretofore. It has also been shown that, the Ryotwaur system, divested of the principle of joint

---

* See Note F.

responsibility, would render the Government revenue insecure. The Ryotwaur plan is, therefore, not applicable to this condition of the people, usurping, as it does, the patronage and management of the waste and uncultivated lands. If so applied, it alters completely the relations of the members of the society to each other; and also ostensibly, but not in reality, to Government.

There appear to be four forms in which a joint village responsibility is commonly found to exist in India, the cultivators, or members, being landlords of the soil. In some provinces of Bengal and of Guzerat, the whole village land is, or has been, occupied by one family, the members of which pay shares of the village assessment according to the extent of their cultivation, or liability, for the year. They seldom change their fields, and elect from among themselves their manager, or Patail, for the year, whose duty it is to make the best possible bargain he can with the agents of Government in respect to the village rental of the year. Another form is, where the Ryots are not tied down to particular fields, but cultivate those that are vacant; the whole produce of the lands of the village, whether from the fields cultivated by the owners, or by tenants at will, or hired labourers, being equally divided among the owners, or families who claim the ownership of the land. A third, and very prevalent mode is, that all the lands of the village are portioned out to from eight to thirty families, or more or less, according to the extent of the village lands. These families never change their lands and estates, and are taxed with the discharge of a certain fixed proportion of the whole village assessment, whatever it may be. In some of these villages the estates are subdivided among the members of the families, and the parcel held by each member being precisely what he is entitled to as an inheritance, it is never changed, and may be sold, mortgaged, or bequeathed, by its occupant. In other villages, the members of each family owning an estate club their means and labour, and divide the returns equally; or some members do so, and some cultivate their own portions marked off to them from the general estate. If several families are ruined, the remaining families are bound, in addition to their own, to pay the shares of the assessment of the defaulting families: but then they may occupy, and in fact do hold, as a corporation, the proprietorship of the estates which have fallen in, and which they let, sell, or mortgage, through their Patail, to assist him in discharging the common impost to Government. By this mode the Patail is generally both a Government and a village servant; and his office is hereditary and seldom elective; he is paid both by Government and by the corporation. A fourth form is, where each individual is landlord of a small estate; but has a joint responsibility in discharging the Government assessment, and a joint interest in the ownership of waste or lapsed lands. I am almost inclined to think that this was the mode prevalent in Canara and Malabar, when we first occupied these countries, and that the Government collectors infringed it, by taking charge of all the unoccupied lands of the village as the property of Government, without at the same time relieving the Ryots from their joint responsibility; but as I have no personal knowledge of these countries, I only suggest the notion for the consideration of others. The village, community, corporation, or municipality, as Mr. Thackeray terms it, is so distinctly recognized in every part of India, that these provinces must certainly be considered as forming singular exceptions, if my surmise is wrong.

From what I have stated it will be remarked, that the Ryotwaur system is not applicable to the condition of Ryots, being landowners, and having a joint responsibility and interest in the village assessment and lands. Its effect, however, if applied to any of the four forms which I have described, would be, with few exceptions, to throw each person on his own means and labour, for the cultivation of a particular spot or field; instead of his being able to command, as before, the assistance of his neighbour's stock and labour, and all the advantages resulting from such a division of labour and appropriation of means. This effect would arise whether the Ryotwaur plan continued to be administered with, or without, the rule of responsibility as far as 10 per cent. for the failure of each other. But, if that rule should be maintained, there is, in addition to these disadvantages, an absolute act of injustice done in the assumption* by Government of the waste and uncultivated land; and if it should be abrogated, independently of the questionable right, even then, of Government to assume these lands, a grievous misfortune would be heaped on every landlord; for the retention by Government of these lands enables it to let them to tenants at will at whatever rates it pleases: and what rates it pleases are well and wofully ascertained to be much less than the village corporation would have rented them at, if indeed it would not have preferred ploughing, sowing, and reaping them, by the employment of its own members and means. The necessary re-

---

* See Note G.

sults are, the removal of tenants from the lands which they theretofore assisted the owners in managing, for the purpose of taking the lands offered to them on better terms by Government; and the ruin of the old proprietors, from their being undersold in the market, and from their inability, in many cases, to go on with their agricultural pursuits to so great an extent as before. That mischievous effects of this nature have extensively occurred from the incautious and unbending introduction of the Ryotwaur plan in Miras villages, and from the assumption by Government of the unoccupied estates and waste lands, is unfortunately no theoretical speculation. The fact is known, and has been proved by the ruin of landlords, and the deterioration of the resources of the State, in those provinces where the experiment has been made. The certain effect of lands being let to tenants at will, at low rates and upon Cowles, has been to oblige the landlords of one village to migrate to another where they might not be personally known, in order to obtain waste land from Government agents, on equal terms with persons formerly tenants of such proprietors as themselves, to enable them at once to carry on the business of life, and to compete with those who produced their ruin. The landlords' own lands being thus deserted, Government assumes the management of them, and lets them at low rates to landlords, perhaps of another village, or to persons who had always before been tenants at will; but, take it in any shape, Government loses his full rent on his lands, either in the form of remissions, or in the depression of the rate at which they are rented. The immediate or ultimate effect, therefore, of the Ryotwaur plan, whether of that with, or of that without, a survey and assessment, upon such a condition of the people, has been, and must continue to be, to bring under-tenants on a par with landlords; to ruin the landlords, so far as bringing them to a level with those who are not such; and to cause a great and permanent reduction in the tax or assessment of land, and a corresponding decrease in the permanent resources of the State: to reduce, in short, the whole agricultural community to one undistinguished herd of impoverished and ignorant labourers, and to injure for years the prosperity of the country and the revenues of Government.

In the second case, where the Ryot, not being an owner of land, is jointly responsible to Government for the failure of other Ryots, Government may impose any rules it pleases. The tenant at will is informed of the terms on which he is allowed to rent a field: if he accepts these terms, he is of course liable to have their observance enforced; and this leads me to remark that the description of Mr. Thackeray, that "a village corporation, community, municipality, "or republic, *which is the proprietor* of the *whole* "*lands* of the village," exists, is totally incompatible with the same body of people having "*no* possessory title to the land, and which does "not even claim it," according to Sir Thomas Munro. It may therefore be concluded from the showing of these writers themselves, that the Ryotwaur settlement is not applicable to any corporation such as is contemplated by Mr. Thackeray, *without abandoning those claims of Government which depend on its existence and continuance.* When the corporation is broken up, however, and the claims which rested on its existence resigned, there would be no obstacle to the application of the Ryotwaur system, divested of its rule of joint responsibility, to the new condition of the Ryots.

I have remarked in villages occupied by tenants at will many circumstances which led me to believe that their lands were, at some former period, owned by landlords. Tracts and provinces, where the tenures are in this state, may have been depopulated by wars, famine, or oppression; or through some erroneous principle respecting the increase of cultivation, the land-owners may have been driven to desert their lands and villages, which would then become occupied by tenants at will. In some places, these tenants at will have been so long established that they have acquired the distinguishing appellation of Cuddeem, old or ancient Ryots; and there is no doubt that they enjoy many of the privileges of landlords, and especially that of hereditary occupancy of particular spots of land. I do not know, indeed, why Government should not, at once, consider agriculturists of this class as the owners by prescriptive right of their fields. That famine is a cause of the ruin of landed proprietors, and of their desertion of their countries and homes, never to return, is known to myself. The old village responsibility, as it existed while the village lands were occupied by land-owners, seems to have kept its ground, or to have been regenerated by the Patails, in many instances, in this new state of the society. The same spirit of rivalry is to be found in such villages, respecting village boundaries and the honour of the community, as in villages composed of proprietors; and they too frequently shed their blood and lost their lives in battles for the ownership of a few fields on, or near, a disputed boundary line; and, in spite of the strong denunciation of such proceedings and punishments awarded for them by our Government, they have continued to this day: —so strong is the feeling of these "*republics*" in respect to their rights, when infringed by any power which they can oppose, even with the loss of lives. Opposition of a similar kind to a Government would of course be futile, and it is never attempted. In such villages, the municipal artisans and servants remained, or were re-instituted, as before. They were paid also, as in ancient times, not by the job, but subsisted at the common expense. They were bound, as in Miras villages, to perform for every member of the community, in their professional capacity, whatever he required to be done at their hands; to make or mend the plough, to make ropes and pots, to wash the clothes, to shave, and provide with shoes every agriculturist. In all my own experience, I never received, nor did I ever hear of a complaint being made to any other public functionary, against these artisans, for the neglect or non-performance of their respective duties; or that they served one Ryot before his turn, or oftener or better than others. It is always their interest that the village shall be well stocked with agriculturists, since they and their families then live so much the better, although they also work harder. The keystone of such communities was the Patail, and the cement, these Bullooties, or artisans.

Such is the Ryotwaur system; and such are the conditions of the people, to which it has been, or may yet be, applied. Viewed as a measure of state policy, it is discreditable to his Majesty's Government to fear to be just to the people, and to advance them in the scale of humanity; even if the chimeras of rebellion and revolution were to become incarnate, and produce the realities. As Lord William Bentinck says, "the happiness of millions depends upon the "decision of this question," and the subject is worthy of the most deliberate consideration. I do not wish his Majesty's ministers to trust, without inquiry, to my views and information; but I entreat them to make inquiry; and to satisfy themselves that one considerable portion of British subjects in India is fast advancing to the lowest scale of human existence, under the operation of a specious plan for maintaining the peace of the countries they inhabit, and their subjection to his Majesty's throne, in a state of Utopian bliss. A collector of the Deccan thus describes the condition of the people of his district, after being several years under the British Government, and the reader will remark the existence in that region of the same circumstances, which Mr. Thackeray so much dwells upon in respect to the Madras territories, the increase of cultivation, and the turning of Peons and all other persons into ploughmen; while it will be distinctly seen how completely the people have thus been thrown back. As the old Ryotwaur plan was then in operation in the Deccan, the heavy and levelling influence of its maxims has accelerated the indigence and barbarism of the inhabitants. But it appears that the retrogradation hitherto of the prosperity of the country is greatly to be attributed to the recent subversion of a native government, to the obstruction of former channels of advancement and prosperity, and to the non-substitution of others, of any thing like equal importance, in their place.

" Notwithstanding," says Mr. Robertson, " the " partial failure of some of the crops (in 1821- " 2,) grain was so abundant in this year, " that it fell to a price unexampled in the " memory of man, or in any record of former " times."—" Even at this rate there was no " market, and no demand. The Ryots had " therefore to contend with great difficulties. " Those who had stacked good crops, could " not convert them into money; and though " ever so abundant, they were scarcely ade- " quate to cover the expenses and demands

" on their owners. Those who had reaped " bad crops were in a still worse condition. " The quantity of grain they had to sell would " bring no return in money, at all adequate " to their family and agricultural obligations " for the year. Those who had had no crops " at all, had had all the expense of cultivating " without any income to balance it. There " was no profit or addition to stock in this " year."—" There was an absurdity in a whole " population shouting out that they were starv- " ing, when grain was so very cheap and abun- " dant, that, however strongly it marks the " trifling degree of credit due to the clamorous " representations of a mob, headed by a few " leading men, it was nevertheless distinctly in- " dicative of the sinking state of the people."— " The people were groping for a cause on " which to fasten the distress occasioned by " influences to them imperceptible; and we " were glad to shut out from our view, by " any veil, their powerful operation. The rights " realized by Patails for two centuries, and ad- " mitted by the people themselves to the very " day of our occupation of the country; these " rights, the essential result, and one of the " strongest supports of the village corporation, " were complained of as injurious, by a people " dwindling into wretchedness from political "causes."—"The consequence of the cheap-"ness of grain, and the general inability of "the people to support themselves and pay "the government dues, during this year, "(1822-3), from the savings of former years, "were the throwing up of lands held by farmers "on leases, and their desertion to the Nizam's "country, and the non-realization of one sixth "part of the whole revenue." In the next year, 1823-4, it appears, that, owing to a failure of the crops, grain became dearer; "but those "who were reduced to sell at a disadvantage in "the preceding year were now little able to "re-purchase the means of subsistence at so "dear a rate."—"Famine seemed to stare us "in the face. Grain was, however, already "abundant, and, considering the times, tole-"rably cheap." In enumerating the causes of this state of things, this collector says, "Among "the greatest of these was the number of Mah-"rattas thrown back on their agricultural rela-"tions. Instead of aiding their Jutha Bhows, "by sending them the savings of their pay, "they now lived upon them, without contri-"buting any thing, or but little, to the common "purse of the family. Unskilled in agriculture, "and without other means of home employ-"ment, what could they do? There was no "service for them as soldiers in foreign states.

" Our own army was chiefly recruited from the " Concans, and our drafts were not increased " since the war. Many converted their swords " into ploughshares, and were the means of " adding considerably to the glut of the market " in 1822, when all were sellers of grain, and " there were few or no consumers, who were " not also producers. The general peace also " in India deprived of employment many per- " sons belonging to the surrounding countries, " and they also had no resource but to follow " the plough. In the time of the Mahrattas, the " quantity of grain produced was much less " from the fewer number of cultivators, and " from the value of grass to a government " whose warlike force was chiefly composed " of horse."—" Those who did grow grain had " therefore a sure market and a good price. " This, together with the savings of many mem- " bers of each family employed by Government, " by all its rich dependents, and by the Soobe- " daurs and Maumletdaurs of Guzerat and the " Carnatic, who, wherever they acquired their " money, spent it at Poona, on marriages and " feasts, and a numerous retinue of Mahratta " servants and dependents, enabled the Deccan " villages, in former times, to be doubly and " trebly assessed, and yet to feel the hardship " of the taxation less than our own moderate "assessments. The contrast cannot fail to "strike every observer. Poona, and the sur-"rounding country, now only presents the tame-"ness of poverty, the apathy of a people with-"out employment, and living without an ob-"ject."—"The intrigues of foreign princes, the "paramount nature of the Paishwa's rule, and "all the sources of emolument attendant on a "court where corruption was openly practised, "fed hundreds who are now only remarkable "for knavery, and who will never be able to "wheel the plough under a semicircle of half "a mile."

The description given in these extracts is in a greater or less degree applicable to every province of India that has come under our subjection. Prosperity withers under our shade. We have grasped and monopolized every thing—the field of honourable ambition, every lucrative post of a great and extensive empire, every road to military fame and advancement; and, by the activity of our free traders, we have superseded even the coarsest manufactures of the country. The business of life has been compressed into its dullest routine; to worship images; to go on pilgrimages; and to grow strong in religious prejudices and immorality, through ignorance and poverty. A barrier has been erected which no man can pass; a weight has been imposed which crushes every one into indigence. The Hindoo can only become rich in religious grace by prayer and fasting; and may possibly acquire a treasure of mental resignation, the boon of Britons to men of dark complexions.

The subjects of the Bengal Presidency are not in a better condition perhaps, viewing them in all relations, than those of Madras. But we have had the honour of failing in that country on principles, and with views, which all men must admire and respect. The liberal, the just Cornwallis has left, to the glory of his Majesty's Government and of his native country, a mark of the true and enlightened policy which should regulate the Government of India. Here we find no errors of right and wrong; his was no scheme to render the wasting influence of our sovereignty more baneful and destructive; not his the timid policy that would reduce the inhabitants of India to slavery and ignorance, that we may sleep securely through our despotism, or fill our coffers by the bodily endurance and mental degradation of whole nations and races of men. That statesman saw the mischiefs of our depressing rule; and when it fell to his lot to meet the views of Lord Melville and the Directors in framing better fiscal arrangements, he grounded his operations on a policy as congenial to his own enlightened mind, as it was satisfactory to the statesmen to whom he was responsible. But that plan also failed, in no small degree from the imperfection of our administration of justice at the time of its adoption; but chiefly because it was in a great degree incompatible with the rights of other men, than those whose interests it established in opposition to theirs. Although the system is, after a long period, now beginning to work better, and to produce happier results, (since, perhaps, it cannot occasion any more mischief,) the benefit has not become sufficiently extensive to allow me to represent the people of Bengal as requiring no attention from the foresight and humanity of his Majesty's Government. Lord Cornwallis's plan has been unjustly censured by one of the first philosophers of the age, upon grounds which, advanced by such a reasoner, deserve the most scrutinizing attention. I cannot therefore pass over, without a few remarks, the following passages from Mill's History of British India, from which it might be inferred that his Lordship had erred in principles rather than in their incautious application.

"The abstract theory," says Mr. Mill, "now "acted upon by the Governor General, namely, "that the highest improvements in the cultiva-"tion of the land can be expected from none

" but the proprietors of the land, was just in " itself, and a truth of no small importance. " But, though proprietors alone have sufficient " motives for the highest efforts in cultivation, " the Governor General and his ministerial and " directorial masters, who concurred with him, " ought to have reflected that there are sorts of " proprietors; and that it is not from every sort " that any improvement whatsoever, or any " attempt towards improvement, is to be ex- " pected. They might have reflected for how " many centuries the soil of Poland has been " private property, or the soil of Russia, and " how little in those countries of any thing like " improvement has yet taken place. They " might have recollected that the nobles even of " France, where knowledge was so far advanced, " had, for many centuries before the revolution, " enjoyed the property of the soil of France, and " that the agriculture of France still continued " in the most deplorable condition. There are " three sets of circumstances whose operation, " where it is felt, prevents the improvement of " the soil at the hands of its proprietors; firstly, " ignorance; secondly, possessions too large; " and, thirdly, too much power over the imme- " diate cultivators. The last is by far the most " important circumstance, because men, with " very few exceptions, as education and govern-

" ment have hitherto moulded their minds, are
" more forcibly drawn by the love of absolute
" power, than by that of money, and have
" greater pleasure in the prostrate subjection of
" their tenants than the increase of their rents.
" When our countrymen draw theories from
" England, it would be good if they understood
" England. It is not because in England we
" have a landed aristocracy that our agriculture
" has improved, but because the laws of England
" afford to the cultivator protection against his
" lord. It is the immediate cultivators who have
" increased so wonderfully the produce of the
" land in England, not only without assistance
" from the proprietors, but often in spite of
" them. The proprietors of the land in Eng-
" land, even to this hour, exhibit one of the
" strongest proofs which can be adduced of the
" ascendancy which is exercised by the love of
" domination over the love of improvement and
" of wealth. No principle is more thoroughly
" established, and indeed more universally ad-
" mitted, than that the grant of leases, and leases
" of a long duration, to the immediate cultiva-
" tors of the soil, are essential to all spirited and
" large improvement. But the proprietors of
" the soil in England complain that leases ren-
" der their tenantry too independent of them,
" and the greater proportion of the land of Eng-

" land is cultivated on tenure at will. If the " gentlemen of England will sacrifice improve- " ment to the petty portion of arbitrary power, " which the laws of England allow them to " exercise over tenants at will, what must we " not expect from the Zemindaurs of Hindoostan, " with minds nurtured to habits of oppression, " when it is referred to themselves whether they " shall or shall not have power over the miser- " able Ryots, to whom the law is too imperfect " to yield any protection."*

" The effect of *ignorance*," continues this writer, " with respect to improvement is too " obvious to require illustration. But it may be " remarked, that it operates with peculiar " efficacy in augmenting the force of the most " powerful of the causes by which the proprie- " tors of land are made to prevent improve- " ment. The love of domination has always the " greatest sway in the most ignorant state of the " human mind."

" The effect of *large possessions* in preventing " those efforts and sacrifices on which improve- " ment depends, deserved profound considera- " tion of the Indian legislator. It cannot

---

* *Mill's History of British India*, Vol. III. Chap. v. Book vi. page 275.

" escape the feeblest powers of reflection, that " the man who enjoys a vast accumulation of " wealth must regard with comparative indif- " ference small acquisitions; and that the pro- " spect of increasing his great revenue by slowly " adding the painful results of improvement can- " not operate very powerfully on his mind. It " is the man of small possessions who feels most " sensibly the benefit of petty accessions. It is " on the immediate cultivator, wherever the " benefit of his improvement is allowed to de- " volve in full upon himself, that the motives to " improvement operate with the greatest force. " That benefit, however, cannot devolve upon " him in full, unless he is the proprietor as well " as the cultivator of his fields; and hence in " part the backwardness of agriculture in some " of the most civilized portions of the globe. " There was an opportunity in India to which " the history of the world presents not a parallel. " Next after the sovereign, the immediate cul- " tivators had by far the greatest portion of " interest in the soil; for the rights (such as " they were) of the Zemindaurs a complete " compensation might have easily been made; " the generous resolution was adopted of sacri- " ficing to the improvement of the country the " proprietary rights of the sovereign. The mo- " tives to improvement which property gives, "and of which the power was so justly appre-"ciated, might have been bestowed upon those "upon whom they would have operated with a "force, incomparably greater than that with "which they could operate upon any other class "of men; they might have been bestowed upon "those from whom alone, in every country, the "principal improvements in agriculture must be "derived, the immediate cultivators of the soil: "and a measure, worthy to be ranked amongst "the noblest that ever was taken for the im-"provement of any country, might have helped "to compensate the people of India for the "miseries of that misgovernment which they "had so long endured. But the legislators were "English aristocrats, and aristocratical prejudices "prevailed."*

It will be remarked at the outset that Mr. Mill, although he does appear to have some faint glimmering† of the truth, makes the same

---

* *Mill's Hist. of India*, Vol. III. Book v. Chap. vi., pages 276 and 277.

† Mr. Mill, in page 273, vol. III. of his *British India*, has the following passage:—"The possessions of the Ryots, either "individually or by villages, were hereditary possessions. So "long as they continued to pay to Government the due pro-"portion of the produce, they could not lawfully be dispos-"sessed. They not only transmitted their possessions by

mistake in reasoning that Lord Cornwallis made in practice, in respect to the inferior holders, or Mirassadaurs, the real owners of the land, and imagines that the Government had a right to overlook their superior title to its possession.

"descent, but had the power of alienation, and could either "sell them or give them away." This is a perfectly true description. But Mr. Mill, in page 271, not only contradicts it in plain terms, but also by inference. "These parties," says Mr. Mill, "shared in the produce of the soil. That "party *to any useful purpose* most properly deserves the "name of proprietor to whom the principal share of the "produce for ever belongs. To him who derives the "smallest share of the produce the title of owner least of all "belongs. In India, *to the Sovereign the profit* of the land "may be said to have wholly belonged. The *Ryot* obtained "a mere *subsistence*, not more than the necessary wages of his "labour."—"To the Government belonged more than one half "of the produce of the soil." Mr. Mill adds in a note, "This is even the language of English law;" and he quotes the proof as follows, "By a grant of *the profits* of the land," say the English lawyers, "the *whole land* itself doth pass. For "what is land but the profits thereof." In the first passage Mr. Mill says, the Ryot is the owner, and in the last that Government is, and can alone be, the owner of the land. In the first passage he says the Ryot can alienate his land by sale or gift, in the second he proves that *the profit*, the only thing which could make it saleable or worth having, is possessed, not by the Ryot, but by the Government. It is evident, therefore, I think, that the historian's notions on this subject were not quite clear.

Had he argued upon the real condition of the Ryots, Mr. Mill could have censured Lord Cornwallis on true grounds of blame, for abolishing or suppressing the reality of Mr. Mill's own theoretical plan, which had an actual existence at the time in the Bengal provinces. The mass of the people were then really both the cultivators and proprietors of their fields; and Lord Cornwallis erred by not discovering, in time, how much they were proprietors. Mr. Mill might have supported his theory by declaiming against the injustice of depriving men of their birth-rights, and on this ground have had ample scope for expatiating on the hastiness and impropriety of his lordship's plan. But, as it is, his arrow has been shot at general principles, instead of the particular measure, as bearing reference to a true state of things, and it remains to be seen with what success.

Mr. Mill admits that the Governor General's theory was *just*, "that the highest improvements "in the cultivation of the land can be expected "from none but the proprietor of the land," and "that this is a truth of no small importance." He then says that there are *sorts* of proprietors; and that the sort he prefers is that in which the cultivator and proprietor are the same person; in short, Sir Thomas Munro's cultivating landlords; the agriculturists of India as we found them in nine cases out of ten. That Mr. Mill could have allowed his acute understanding to be clouded in the consideration of this question, by his prejudices against aristocrats, is a clear proof of the proneness of human nature to be led into error from preconceived notions. Propounding his abstract theory, and with his mind divested, perhaps for the moment, of those prejudices, this is what Mr. Mill says—" If sales " went on, it being the nature of land, as of " other property, to change hands continually, the " whole land would be divided at last into very " small portions, covered by a dense population, " no portion of which would be in circum- " stances much better than those of the " labourers. Is this in itself a desirable state of " things? Is it either followed or preceded by " a desirable state of things?"

" All the blessings," continues Mr. Mill, " which flow from that grand and distinguished " attribute of our nature, its progressiveness, the " power of advancing continually from one de- " gree of knowledge, one degree of command " over the means of happiness to another, seem " in a great measure to depend upon the exist- " ence of a class of men who have their time at " their command, that is, who are rich enough " to be freed from all solicitude with respect to " the means of living in a certain state of enjoy-

"ment" (literary aristocrats.) "It is by this "class of men that knowledge is cultivated and "enlarged; it is also by this class that it is "diffused: it is this class of men whose chil- "dren receive the best education, and are pre- "pared for all the higher and more delicate "functions of society, as legislators, judges, "administrators, teachers, inventors in all the "arts, and superintendents in all the more im- "portant works, by which the dominion of the "human species is extended over the power of "nature."

"For the happiness, therefore, as well as the "ornament of our nature, it is peculiarly de- "sirable that a class of this description should "form as large a proportion of each community "as possible. For this purpose it is absolutely "necessary that population should not, by a "forced accumulation of capital, be made to go "on till the return to capital from the land is "very small."*

The sophistry of the assertion, that the proprietors of the soil ought also, in order to advance their happiness and improvement, to be its cultivators, is thus exposed by Mr. Mill himself on true and general principles. Mr. Mill

---

* *Mill's Elem. of Pol. Econ.*, pages 62, 63, and 64.

talks of the *motives* to make improvements being likely to operate with a force incomparably greater on petty landlords than on any other sort. Admitting this to be true, though I shall show that it is not, how does he reconcile this theory with that other respecting the division of labour? "So obvious is this advantage (the "division of labour) that some remarkable cases "of the division of labour are exemplified in the "earliest stages of the arts."* Yet, in the face of this obvious advantage, the man who owns the land is the best person to sow, plough, and reap it. He is to go to the market himself to sell his produce. He must attend to his cattle, and do every thing himself without assistance. Compare this condition of Mr. Mill's proprietors with that of Mr. Mill's savages, "who even in the "simplest state of labour, when, if one man "should confine himself to the operation of "climbing trees for their fruit, another to the "operations of ensnaring and killing animals, "they would acquire a dexterity greater than "they would have acquired had each occasion-"ally performed both operations, and would by "such means obtain a greater abundance, both "of fruit and of game."† And whence is the

* *Mill's Elem. of Pol. Econ.*, page 13.

† *Ibid.*, pages 12 and 13.

capital to be derived for great improvements, or even for "any improvement whatsoever" by such a set of cultivating proprietors? Mr. Mill admits that capital is requisite for improvements. In truth, it is as much required as *motives.* Without it, motives will remain inert:—then, if a small proprietor has no capital, let him be ever so desirous, he cannot by any possibility improve his land: but a larger proprietor, who, we may admit, has capital, can by possibility do so; he can do so, if he has the will. In the one case, therefore, improvement *cannot* take place, in the other *it may;* and I shall show that it often has done so.

But I shall first advert to the maxim that the cultivating proprietors have motives to improvement, which act upon them with incomparably greater force than upon any other class of men. On this subject I might give my sentiments in my own words, but I prefer clothing them in those of writers whose merits are established, and who are well known to Mr. Mill and the public; since the opinions of such men may carry much greater weight with them, than might be accorded to mine. The Edinburgh Reviewers justly allege, that "every system, "which has for its object to enforce an equal "division of landed property, must necessarily "occasion too great an increase of agricultural

" population; and must also operate to reduce " landed property into such minute portions as " will neither afford sufficient employment to " the families occupying them, nor allow of " their being cultivated in the most improved " and cheapest manner."* " In no country of " Europe (France is alluded to) is there such " a vast body of proprietors; and in no civilized " European country, with the single exception " of Ireland, is there so large a proportion of " the population directly engaged in the culti- " vation, or rather, we should say, the torture " of the soil. And yet the system is only in its " infancy. Should it be supported in its present " vigour, for another half century, *la grande* " *nation* will certainly be the greatest pauper- " warren in Europe, and will, along with Ire- " land, have the honour of furnishing hewers of " wood and drawers of water for all the other " countries of the world."† The reader will, I hope, readily recognize the exact parallel that exists between India and France. The laws of succession to, and subdivision of, property, are now nearly the same in both countries. France exhibits a recent example of the theories of

---

* *Edinburgh Review*, No. LXXX. page 362.

† *Ibid.* No. LXXX. page 369.

Mr. Mill and Sir Thomas Munro. India, in nine tenths of its extent, presents us with a practical example of its effects after an experiment of ages. "But," continue the Reviewers, "in the "great majority of cases, they will continue to "reside on the little properties they have re-"ceived from their ancestors; and the process "of division and subdivision will continue, until "the whole land has been parcelled out into "patches, and filled with an agricultural po-"pulation, destitute alike of the means and "desire of rising in the world."* Why they should be destitute of the desire of rising in the world, is accounted for by the Reviewers in another article from which I have already quoted. "Economy is in no respect different from the "other virtues; and it would be unreasonable "to expect that it should be strongly manifested, "where it does not bring along with it a corre-"sponding reward. Before a man can accumu-"late he must live; and if the sum that remains "to him after his necessary expenses are de-"ducted be but small and trifling, the proba-"bility is that he will rather choose to consume "it immediately, than to hoard it up in the "expectation, that by the addition of further

---

* *Edinburgh Review*, No. LXXX. page 362.

"savings, it may, at some future and very distant "period, become the means of making a small "addition to his income. In a state of indi-"gence there is neither the power *nor the wish* "*to save.*"*—"This fact," say the Reviewers, alluding to a statement of M. Garnier, whose authority they deem to be unquestionable, "is "pregnant with information; and with infor-"mation, we regret to say, that gives the most "unfavorable view possible of the state of "France. It proves that agriculture is not pro-"secuted in that kingdom as it is prosecuted in "England, for the sake of realizing a profit on "the capital employed in carrying it on, but in "order to acquire the means of existence."† Such is precisely the state of India, and such is the condition to which Sir Thomas Munro was desirous of bringing all those inhabitants of it, for whom he held in his hands the power of raising almost any edifice of civilization that he might choose to erect. Such are the practical results of Utopian plans like that of Mr. Mill, originating in prejudice; such are *the motives* he descants upon as operating so powerfully on the improvement of the people and the increase of national wealth!

---

* *Edinburgh Review*, No. LXXIX. page 5.

† *Ibid*, No. LXXX, p. 366.

It might not be necessary to examine any further the creed advanced by Mr. Mill in the extracts I have given from his History of India, but, as the subject is before me, and as the false reasoning he has adduced may not strike every casual reader, it will not, I hope, be deemed irrelevant to probe his arguments a little deeper.

"There are three sets of circumstances whose "operation, where it is felt, prevents the im-"provement of the soil at the hands of its pro-"prietors: firstly, ignorance; secondly, possessions "too large; and thirdly, too much power over "the immediate cultivators." In respect to the first of these checks, Mr. Mill must be perfectly satisfied that ignorance, while it operates, will operate as strongly against one sort of proprietors as against another; and I have already shown that he himself thinks its removal least problematical, and in a great measure to depend even "upon the existence of a class of men "who have time at their command." This check therefore was liable to, and might be removed under Lord Cornwallis's plan; but there is not a possibility of its removal under Mr. Mill's. The second and third preventives may be considered only so far operative, as that, where the laws do not adequately provide for the protection of farmers and cultivators, they might, if the landlords neglected their own interests, occasion oppression to be suffered by those classes: but they do not of necessity do so; nor would they at all, if the proprietor were wise enough to discover that the well-being of these classes promoted his own. Besides, great proprietors have what is totally wanting to cultivating proprietors; they possess, or at least may if they please possess, capital, and thence the power of making improvements, if they will; but, having capital and will at their command, *ignorance alone* can prevent them from increasing their incomes, whether with the design of opposing, as feudal Barons, their prince, or of fluttering in luxurious splendour, the gaudy butterflies of a modern court. Does Mr. Mill mean to say that noblemen and great proprietors of land do not know full well, now, as in former times, the use of money or capital (or by whatever name wealth can be designated) in securing that domination, the love of which is so powerful a motive in his estimation; or that, aware of this mean to an end so eagerly sought after, they would pass it over in neglect, or with contempt? The second check to improvement cannot, therefore, I imagine, be said to be applicable to Lord Cornwallis's plan, or to annul the truth in regard to *his* sort of priprietors, "that the highest improvement in the culti-"vation of the land is to be expected from "none but from the proprietors,"—a maxim which Mr. Mill admits to be "just in itself," —and the observance or proof of which, I must repeat, was practicable with such a sort of proprietors as Lord Cornwallis created; but which is not practically possible to such a sort as Mr. Mill recommends. It is true, however, that for the *highest* degree of improvement, estates may be *too large and unwieldy,* and that nearly as great a mistake may be made by the creation of *too large* as of *too small* estates:—but certainly of the two, there can be no question regarding which is the most likely to tend to the improvement of agriculture and the increase of capital, in the best proportioned ratio to the increase of population. Lord Cornwallis, however, did not change, in respect to the estates he formed, the Hindoo law of inheritance and subdivision of property; so that, even if his estates were too large at first, which in most instances they really were not, they would soon have become split into as small estates as even Mr. Mill could desire. The third check to improvement, "too much power over the cultivators," is alleged to produce its effect by the oppression of these cultivators; but the most probable effect, in my opinion, of any want of due protection, under such circumstances, from by the laws to the lower classes, appears to be that, if the greater proprietors were sufficiently well informed to be aware how they could improve their estates, they would probably be oppressive to their vassals in effecting such improvement at their hands, and at least that they assuredly would not oppress them *to prevent* their own advantage. Where Mr. Mill's first check, "*ignorance*," was not operative, therefore, oppression might be a mean, but certainly not the check, to improvement. As for the rest, *the laws*, by Mr. Mill's own admission, are to be blamed, and not the frame-work of the society.

Mr. Mill has assumed to himself a dictatorship for knowledge of England and English institutions. He plainly tells us that Lord Cornwallis was ignorant of them; and that nobody but himself knew or knows any thing of England. I myself shall not enter the lists with Mr. Mill on this point, but there are other philosophical dictators in England besides Mr. Mill, and I shall show what doctrines they have promulgated; and at least prove that Mr. Mill knows less of England than Lord Cornwallis did. But, before I show his deficiency of information, I shall expose this philosopher's inconsistent reasonings upon his own premises. "It "is not," he says, "because in England we have "a landed aristocracy that our agriculture has "improved, but because the laws of England "offered to the cultivator protection against his "lord."—And why, I would ask, might not the laws of India be made to afford protection to the Indian Ryot against the Indian lord? By such an argument does Mr. Mill prove that there is a defect in the machine itself? or only, that if it is not properly put together in all its parts, it will not work well? On the same ground he might argue, that a clock, having all its wheels and parts perfect, was useless in itself, because *he* or Lord Cornwallis could not, or did not, put them properly together so as to make the machine tell the hour. If his position proves any thing, it proves that, with good laws and an aristocracy, England *has improved*. Mr. Mill then distinctly states,—first,—that the wonderful improvements in English agriculture are attributable solely to the cultivators—secondly, that it is essential *to all* spirited and *large* improvement that the cultivators should have long leases,—thirdly, that long leases are *not* granted by the proprietors of England. He, in fact, first alleges that wonderful improvements have occurred in England, and then proves that they were impossible! It might be put to the experience of any person who has ever been in India, whether the Indian mode of cultivation is in any respect to be compared to that of England. Yet, in India, possessing the advantage of a climate genial to the productions of the earth, of a soil easily worked, (compared with that of England,) of a body of the smallest proprietors, precisely such as Mr. Mill in his theory contemplates, and whose ancestors have, for ages, enjoyed in perfection Mr. Thackeray's Utopian happiness of a country life, of a government at present mild and humane to a proverb, and above all, of having no aristocrats — possessing all these advantages real and philosophical—what do we see? Nothing but misery—nothing but human beings struggling for the means of existence. What a difference between the two countries! the country of cultivating proprietors, and the country of aristocrats! "But," says Mr. Mill, "England is cultivated by the tenants "at will of an aristocracy;" and again, "England has wonderfully improved in agriculture." What would any man of common sense, who had ever heard of Aristotle, infer from two such assertions? Would it not be, that "England "has wonderfully improved in agriculture, from "being cultivated by the tenants at will of an "aristocracy." I admit that good laws have tended to produce such a state of things as to allow of these assertions being made;—but give the same or as good laws to any other nation, and will Mr. Mill prove that the same result will not occur?

Mr. Mill speaks of Poland and Russia in exemplification of his opinions; but as, by adverting to the advancement of knowledge in France, he leads us to suppose that he is willing to admit these other countries to be in a state of ignorance, (*expressio unius est exclusio alterius,*) it will not perhaps be considered that I assume too much, after what I have already said respecting ignorance as a check to improvement, to impute the backwardness of these two countries to ignorance. We have, therefore, only France remaining, conjointly with England, as an instance among those adduced still applicable to this discussion. "The prejudices," say the dictators from whom I have already quoted, "of most political "philosophers against the custom of primogeni-"ture, seem to us to rest on no solid foundation." Dr. Smith says that it is a custom which, "in "order to enrich one beggars all the rest of the "children."——"But, so far from agreeing in "this opinion, we cannot help thinking that it is "to this very custom that much of the industry, "wealth, freedom, and civilization of modern "Europe are to be ascribed; and that, were it "abolished, and a system of equal division of "landed property established in its stead, all the "children of landlords, the oldest as well as the "youngest, would be reduced to a state of com-"parative poverty, at the same time that the "prosperity of the other classes would be greatly

" impaired."*—" We are disposed to think," say the same writers, " that the state and magnifi-" cence in which our great landed proprietors " live, act as powerful incentives to the industry " and enterprize of the mercantile and manufac-" turing classes, who never think they have " accumulated a sufficient fortune until they are " able to emulate the splendour of the landlords; " whereas, had these great properties been frit-" tered down by the scheme of equal division " among children, the standard of competence " would have been lowered universally, and " there would in consequence have been less " exertion in all classes of the community."

" That the condition of the agricultural classes " in France has been considerably improved " since the revolution is unquestionable. But it " is not true that this improvement has been in " any respect owing to the law of equal inherit-" ance. It has taken place not in consequence " of that law, but in despite of it. The abolition " of the feudal privileges of the nobility and " clergy, and of the *gabelle, corvées,* and other " grievously oppressive and partial burdens and " imposts, would of themselves have rendered " the proprietors and farmers a great deal more

---

* *Edinburgh Review*, No. XL. page 360.

"respectable."*—"Every one knows," say again the Reviewers, "that Normandy has always "been one of the richest and best cultivated "provinces of France; and yet Normandy is "one of those provinces in which, under the old "*regime*, the law of primogeniture had the most "extensive and general operation. But, instead "of being improved, there is undoubted evidence "to show that the agriculture and general ap- "pearance of the province is rapidly changing "for the worse under the existing law of succes- "sion."† We thus learn, in contradiction to Mr. Mill's assertions and opinions, that the most thriving country of France was that in which great properties were preserved by the most extensive operation of the law of primogeniture; and that, if the French *had had the knowledge* requisite for making improvements, *their love of money*, exemplified in the imposition of oppressive taxes, *would* have stimulated them to make improvements in agriculture; and we also have a well drawn picture of the baneful effects of a society of cultivating proprietors on the advancement of national wealth and human happiness.

"In a country like England," continue these

---

* *Edinburgh Review*, Vol. XL. page 364.

† *Ibid.* Vol. XL. page 367.

writers, "where a highly improved system of "husbandry is generally introduced, where "farms are extensive, and the most powerful "machinery is employed in agricultural opera-"tions, only a proportionally small number of "the inhabitants are employed in the cultivation "of the soil."——"The national wealth and the "comfort of all classes are prodigiously aug-"mented in consequence of this division of "employments."——"A spirit of industry is "thus universally diffused, and that apathy and "languor which are characteristic of a rude state "of society entirely disappear. No one will "presume to say that the agriculture of France "is in nearly so improved a state as that of "Britain; that it is not in fact a hundred years "behind ours; and yet, while there are more "than two thirds of the people of France em-"ployed in this inferior cultivation, less than "one-third of our people suffice to carry on "the infinitely superior system of cultivation "adopted in this country."——"Let us of Eng-"land then," say these able writers, "not there-"fore, by giving the smallest countenance to "any scheme, either for dividing estates, or for "building cottages on wastes, do any thing that "might by possibility tend to increase the purely "agricultural population of the country."*

---

* *Edinburgh Review*, Vol. XL. pages 370, 371, and 372.

Mr. Mill, in citing England, ancient France, and Russia and Poland, on the one hand, should have dealt fairly with us, and quoted Ireland and modern France on the other. We should thus have seen both sides of the picture, and probably have differed in opinion from Mr. Mill, as to which was the front of it. The Reviewers, after stating that the Irish proprietor of ten or fifteen acres of land had been obliged to resort to an inferior species of food, remark, " and such too, " we observe, are the consequences now actually " resulting from the same cause in France. That " country is threatened with the double curse of " a redundant and a potatoe-feeding popula- " tion." The following is an unanswerable argument in my judgment:—" A farmer can never " calculate with certainty on the renewal of his " lease. Unless he has accumulated some " capital, he is always exposed to the risk of " being thrown destitute on the world; but it is " not so with the small proprietor, he relies for " support, *not on capital*, but on *land*."* Again the Reviewers say, " It is an *indisputable fact*, " that those countries of Scotland, Kinross for " example, where property is very much divided, " and the proprietors consequently poor, are " very much behind in their agriculture, and are " farmed in a much inferior style to those whose

---

* *Edinburgh Review*, Vol. XL. page 374.

" estates and farms are more extensive."* I shall conclude these quotations from the Edinburgh Reviewers with one more extract. " Far " from joining in the outcry that has been so " frequently raised against the magnitude of the " property in the hands of the aristocracy, we " consider the existence of a numerous and " powerful body of landed proprietors, without " artificial privileges, but possessed of great " natural influence, as essentially contributing to " the improvement and stability of the public " institutions of such densely peopled countries " as France and England; and as forming the " best attainable check to arbitrary power on the " one hand, and to popular frenzy and licentious" ness on the other." Coming from the chair of the Edinburgh dictators, these sentiments may be deemed by Mr. Mill himself to be conclusive against his censure of the principles on which Lord Cornwallis founded his plan of a permanent settlement in Bengal: but the subject is so important, and involves so deeply the interests of millions, that I shall be excused perhaps for adding the opinions of other doctors of an opposite school, who may be said to divide public approbation with their opponents in most political

---

* *Edinburgh Review*, Vol. XL. page 374.

discussions. In fact, the coincidence in the sentiments of these philosophers is one of the strongest arguments I can adduce in favour of their truth and excellence.

"How malignant then, how basely malignant," say the Quarterly Reviewers, "is the conduct of "those who systematically hold up the land-"owners of this country to public obloquy, as "useless drones, fattening from generation to "generation upon the industry of the people! "If they had not from time to time laid out "their capital in the amelioration of the soil, the "produce of land would not have exceeded its "amount in a state of nature; and the increased "population, which in this country finds profit-"able employment in agriculture, as well as in "manufactures and commerce, could not have "been subsisted. Such are the facts." *—"Those "who are not at all conversant with matters of "this nature, are well aware that in former times "the land in this country was greatly subdivided "among a numerous race of unskilful cultiva-"tors. The occupier of thirty or forty acres was "reckoned an opulent and substantial farmer. "Assisted by the members of his family, he per-"formed in person all the labour required on his

---

* *Quarterly Review* for Oct. 1827, pages 412 and 413.

" farm; he fabricated with his own hands all the " clumsy and inefficient instruments employed by " him in husbandry, except perhaps the plough."* " Manufactures and commerce then," continue the Reviewers, " in the modern acceptation of " these terms, were carried on to a very limited " extent among our ancestors; indeed, no foun- " dation existed on which they could have been " raised. The produce obtained by constant " cropping and an unskilful system of tillage " was extremely scanty; it was almost entirely " consumed within the precincts of the farm: " there was little or no surplus left for the land- " lord under the denomination of rent; and the " few taxes imposed for the exigencies of the " State formed a heavy burden difficult to be " borne." (Page 415.) " It is this surplus remaining " after the consumption of the men and the " animals actually engaged in the labour of agri- " culture has been provided for, which forms the " basis of trade and manufactures. Without this " surplus they could not even exist: and in pro- " portion to the increase or diminution of this " surplus will manufactures and commerce flour- " ish or decay." (Page 420.) " Every discovery, " therefore, which augments the gross produce " of land, in a greater ratio than the food con-

---

* *Quarterly Review*, for Oct. 1827, page 414.

"sumed in cultivating it, or which reduces the "quantity consumed in agriculture, while the "gross produce is not diminished, must add to the "surplus which can be expended on manufac-"tures."——"In France, the land is divided into "small farms, among a numerous race of cultiva-"tors, who not only perform the agricultural la-"bour of their fields, but also fabricate at home "by far the greater portion of those articles, which "the corresponding classes in this country de-"rive from public manufactures."——"Twice "the number of men and animals engaged in "tilling a given extent of land in England, are "employed in cultivating an equal extent in "France." (Page 421.)

Such have been the schemes devised for the administration of India. The one created a local gentry by the sacrifice of the rights of the real owners of the land; the other perpetuated poverty and ignorance where a gentry might have been raised. The Bengal plan must tend to improve the condition of the people, until the estates, by the operation of the Hindoo law of succession to property, come to be broken up into little patches belonging to small proprietors, and then every thing will retrograde, or at least stand still at the point of improvement, to which the capital and exertions of the present great proprietors may make an advance. This plan, therefore, may admit of some increase to the national wealth for a certain period of time. The Madras system can only operate, in ninety-nine cases out of a hundred, by increasing a beggarly and ignorant population, without improving the resources of the State, until famine, disease, and wretchedness, sweep off millions, and leave the rest and the Government worse off than at present.

Next in importance to the management of the revenue are the effects produced on the society of India by systems for the administration of justice. It was hardly to be hoped that free-born Englishmen would at once discover and adopt, in the judicial department, a suitable medium to maintain the respectability of the local gentry, and at the same time dispense equal justice to all the people. The feelings of an Englishman, his humanity and civilization, were opposed to the consideration and practice of any plan, that should not unreservedly secure even-handed justice to one man as well as to another, not only in reality, but also in appearance. It was a fortunate circumstance incident to these feelings that, while they operated in withdrawing from us the affections of men of wealth, rank, or influence, they secured to us the respect, at least, of the mass of the people, for our good intentions. If there is in India any ground at all of fidelity and attachment to his Majesty's Government, it is that we wish to deal justly and equally with all men. We have endeavoured, and in some places succeeded, in emancipating the poor from the thraldom of the rich; and we clear our consciences of the lesser evil of degrading the gentry by reflecting on the design or reality of the greater good.

But the greater good might have been equally well, if not better, secured, without incurring so much of the lesser evil; and this is the rock on which we have split in this department of the Government. Like Sir Thomas Munro's revenue plan, the judicial system introduced into India, has, excepting in a few provinces, contributed to reduce the people to one level: but then there is a wide difference in the motives in which the two schemes originated. The revenue plan set out with the desire of effecting the degradation of respectable men, in order that the British Government might remain free from intelligent domestic foes. The judicial plan launched us on a sea of philanthropy and right feeling, and our intentions were founded in justice and honour. The one plan was disgraceful to us as Britons, and as civilized men; the other did us honour, and met with the respect of those even who hated us for its adoption. But the magnanimous Elphinstone has shown to India and to Britain, that justice can be administered to the poor without infringing the privileges and rank of the rich. That accomplished statesman has erected a never decaying monument to his fame, and to the honour of the nation, in the laws which he framed for his petty Government of Bombay, and for the subjects of the Deccan who are subordinate to that Government. They are such as Mr. Mill himself, prejudiced as he is in many cases against India, and (with great justice) against law and lawyers, and forms and technicalities, will be inclined to admire.

With the exceptions I have mentioned, I cannot better elucidate this part of my subject than by reiterating the opinions of some men of sound judgment and great experience, who have favoured the Indian Government with their unreserved sentiments. These sentiments may be accepted as still bearing reference to the present, and perhaps also to future time. They appear, to me at least, to be so faithful a picture, generally speaking, of the present, that although they were written some twenty or thirty years ago, and are only descriptive of the state of things in particular places, and within a limited range, I prefer giving the language of these gentlemen to remodelling their opinions (which are also mine) in my own. Truth is truth still, let who will describe or show it to us.

In Sir Henry Strachey's "Answers to Interrogatories," circulated by Lord Wellesley in January, 1802, are the following passages. "It is not "easy to say whether the moral character of the "natives has improved by means of the system "established by us. In my opinion the system "has little direct influence on the morals of the "people. They are probably somewhat more "licentious than formerly. Chicanery and "subornation, fraud and perjury, are certainly "more common. Oppression, cruelty, and vio-"lence of all sorts, except that of *decoits* and "*choars*, are grown much less frequent. The "ill treatment of women, of servants, and slaves, "has nearly ceased. The same may be said of "the corporal severities formerly exercised in "collecting the revenues. The poor look up to "the laws, and not as heretofore to a patron, for "protection. In some respects, therefore, the "present mode of administering justice may be "deemed conducive to good morals. (*Ans. to* "*Inter*. 15, par. 1st.) I beg leave to offer it as "my opinion that little morality is learned in any "court of justice. In Calcutta, I have reason "to believe, the morals of the people are worse, "in spite of the severity of the police and of the "English laws. Nor do I attribute this solely "to the size, population, and indiscriminate so-"ciety of the capital; but in part to the Supreme

"Court. I scarcely ever knew a native con-"nected with the Supreme Court, whose morals "and manners were not contaminated by that "connexion. In mentioning this evil, which I "by no means attribute to individuals, I trust "it will not be imagined I mean to speak "generally with disrespect of the institution of "the Court itself." (*Ans. to Inter.* 15, par. 3d.) "It will probably be found on inquiry that the "natives do not ascribe the present wretched "state of the old Zemindaurs to the unexpected "difficulty of collecting their revenue under our "regulations, or to other causes of a similar "kind, which are unquestionably the true ones. "They imagine it to be the result of a settled "premeditated plan of policy in the Govern-"ment, to level and degrade its most powerful "subjects." (*Ans. to Inter.* 16, par. 4th.)—— "But the increasing poverty of the higher orders, "and other causes, have contributed to make the "digging and clearing of Tanks very uncommon, "except in towns and a few other places, where "they are least wanted. In this district there "are very few new works of this nature; but the "remains of the old ones attest the superior "opulence of former times; at least they show "that property was more unequally divided "among the natives than at present."——"The "situation of the lower orders is, on the whole,

"somewhat improved by our system of adminis-
"tration; but their nature is not changed. They
"are always in debt, and borrow at enormous
"interest. They are not stimulated to any
"efforts of industry by the security they enjoy,
"but solely by the calls of hunger."——"To
"their few wants, the uniformity and extreme
"simplicity of their habits, their unsocial educa-
"tion, and the heat of the climate; to these
"causes, and not to our laws, are, in my opinion,
"to be ascribed the peculiarities of the people."
—"The condition of the Ryots is, on the whole, I
"think, better, because their lives and limbs are
"safe from the Zemindaurs and collectors of
"revenue. On the other hand, the dread of
"*decoits*, the expense of prosecutions, and the
"spirit of prosecuting, the slowness of our legal
"proceedings, and the doubtfulness of the event
"of lawsuits on account of perjury and other
"causes;—all these are evils of the present day."
(*Ans. to Inter.* 17th.) "Compared with the old
"native Governments, the English Government
"is a good one, inasmuch as it secures the
"country from invasion, and, on the whole, very
"well preserves the lower orders, that is to say,
"the main body of the community, from the
"tyranny of the higher orders. It is scarcely pos-
"sible that much real attachment and loyalty to
"the ruling power can subsist among the higher

" classes. *The total want of energy and spirit, the " poverty and ignorance of the people* compose, in " my opinion, *the strength* of our Government."*
——" Great population and poverty produce " misery and crimes; particularly in a country " where there is no public, and consequently no " certain and regular, provision for the poor; " where there are, I may almost say, more poor " than in any country; and where the ability " and disposition of private individuals to support " them are continually diminishing."——" The " Ryots are now, though more independent, much " worse protected from distress than heretofore. " They once looked up to their Talookdaurs, " who could assist them, and who did to the " utmost of their power; for it was their interest. " The Ryots now have no protector but the " regulations; and the regulations, though they " may serve to defend them, in some measure, " from violence and barbarity, will not feed " them." (*Answers to 18th and 21st Questions.*)
" There is here, as elsewhere, a very numerous " class of the lower orders, ready to serve under " any standard where they can get subsistence.

---

* I would add, and also the disgrace—that the British Government in the nineteenth century should trust to the poverty and ignorance of the people as the pillars of its existence!

"These have no idea of loyalty or disloyalty, "except to the masters who support them. "They would readily enlist with a foreign "power; but I do not call them disaffected, "because custom and necessity lead them to "hire themselves to any master who may be "able to maintain them."——"An institution, or "measure of Government founded merely on "European customs, must be useless and unintel- "ligible."——"The Sepoys are, like the rest of "the natives, entirely uninstructed as to the form "of the Government, of the policy of their rules, "and of the justice of their wars. *It is in this* "*ignorance and apathy that our strength consists.*" ——"With respect to the eligibility of confer- "ring titles and honours on the natives, it might "possibly, if practicable, be of use. It might "serve to attach them to the Government, and "to make them hold themselves in estimation. "But how such an arrangement is to be brought "about, I have no conception."——"On whom, "I beg leave to ask, can titles be conferred, "when none are placed in a situation where it is "possible to render themselves eminent or con- "spicuous? How can their merits be known "when their rulers have no connexion with "them? when there is no intermediate class "between the sovereign power and the common "people?"——"No native can greatly distin-

" guish himself as a soldier, for he can never " rise beyond the rank of a Soobedaur."—— " Men in learned professions have, if possible, " still less opportunity of recommending them- " selves to us."——" I content myself with ob- " serving, that any measure, which would secure " to Government the services of a considerable " number of the most respectable members of " the community, must prove, in many points of " view, beneficial. The Zemindaurs, it will be " recollected, possessed under the native Go- " vernment a degree of power nearly propor- " tionate to their property. Although that " power was perhaps not formally recognized, " nor regularly exerted; still, they did possess a " considerable degree of military, civil, and fiscal " power. They kept their dependents in a state " of union, and were by that means enabled to " protect them, and maintain themselves. At " present, such as have survived the almost " universal destruction of Zemindaurs, are, in " conformity to our notions, reduced to the same " condition, and placed at an equal distance " from us, with the lowest Ryots. Any measure " that has a tendency towards the restoration " of this power, must, I think, advance a step " towards the creation of a body of gentry, who " may perform great services to the public.

"Such a measure would bring the lower orders "more distinctly under the eye of the magistrate. "It might enable us, in some slight degree, to "excite awe, to impress restraint, to awaken "national ardour and love for the Government. "Our moral impotence to produce any effect of "this nature on the minds of the people, which "is at present sufficiently apparent, might be, I "think, if not removed, at least gradually dimin- "ished. To the propriety of any plan that would "invest the higher orders with a liberal au- "thority, that would encourage and enable them "to act without fear in concurrence with Go- "vernment officers for the public good, I beg "leave to subscribe my humble opinion."—— "Some are of opinion that the more power the "natives have, the more they abuse it; that they "are utterly unfit for any but the lowest employ- "ments; and that, however great their salaries, "moderation and disinterestedness can never be "expected from them. This appears to me a mere "fallacy."——"The vices and the crimes of the "people proceed from their poverty and igno- "rance; and I do not consider they are likely to "grow much richer or wiser while the present "state of things exists."——"This assertion, "however, that the vices and crimes of the "people proceed from their poverty and igno-

" rance, I would wish to be understood with " limitations."——" It is not always, therefore, " that the people are worse where they are the " poorest and most ignorant. Nevertheless, the " assertion is, in my opinion, generally speaking, " true."——" It is the principle of ignorance, and " not of fear, that at present preserves us; and, I " should imagine, it will be only when European " laws, religion, and literature, come to be dis- " seminated in this country, that it will be " necessary to draw the reins tighter, and to " show that we certainly, at present, possess " power irresistible to command obedience." ——" But this sort of power, the result of policy " and force on the one hand, and utter ignorance " and wretchedness on the other, does not sup- " pose any influence whatever over the hearts of " the natives." (*Answers to Inter.* 32, 33, and 34.) After deprecating the effects of the intercouse which the natives of Calcutta have with Europeans, and the officers of the King's Court, Sir Henry says, " Moreover, I would appeal to those " who, from their situation or habits, are accus- " tomed to consider these matters with attention, " whether there have not, of late years, been " introduced, and exclusively established, pro- " fessions heretofore almost unknown, namely, " those of informers, sharpers, intriguers, subor- " ners, and false witnesses; whose sole occupa-

" tion is that of preying on their fellow-creatures, " and whose long career of impunity convinces " them that honesty is the worst policy." (*Ans. to Inter*. 34, par. 9th.)

On the subject of criminal justice, this experienced and wise officer observes, " Without " doubt, the present mode of conducting trials is " more regular, satisfactory, and decorous. The " record is properly kept and made up, and every " thing is conducted with fairness and humanity " towards the prisoner: nor could we reconcile " it to ourselves to recur, in any degree, to the " native mode of trial: yet I am inclined to " think that an intelligent native is better " qualified to preside at a trial, than we can " ever be ourselves; and a very few simple rules " would perhaps suffice to correct the abuses of " former times." Speaking of the native commissioner of civil justice, he remarks—" He de- " cides with the greatest ease a vast number of " causes. He is perfectly acquainted with the " language, the manners, and even the person " and characters, of all who come before him. " Hence perjury is very uncommon in his court." " I am fully convinced that a native of common " capacity will, after a very little experience, " examine witnesses, and investigate the most " intricate case, with more temper and perse- " verance, with more ability and effect, than

" almost any European."——" I cannot help " wishing that these situations were more respectable in a pecuniary view, and that they " were empowered to decide causes to almost " any amount."——" Should it here occur that " very few, if any, are qualified, from habit and " education to pronounce a decision, or to comprehend a complicated judicial case; that the " range of their ideas is too narrow; that their " minds are cramped, and that they possess not " that vigour and perseverance, and those enlarged views, which would enable them to " perform the duty of judges:—if there is any " one of this opinion, I would take the liberty " to ask, How it is possible the natives in general " should, in the miserably subordinate and servile employments to which they are confined, " have qualified themselves better? I would " observe how very easily they all acquire the " requisite qualifications for the duties which we " are pleased to entrust to them. I would ask, " who can doubt that they would very shortly, if " not depressed and dispirited, become at least " equal to the functions they performed before " we came among them?"—" I confess it is my " wish, though possibly I may be blamed for " expressing it, not only to have the authority " of the natives as judges extended, but to see " them, if possible, enjoy important and confi-

" dential situations in other departments of the " State."

I am almost ashamed to confess that the wisdom which pervades Sir Henry Strachey's reports has been neglected to this hour. Seldom indeed it is, that men in his situation can be expected so far to divest themselves of a fellow-feeling towards their own services, as to recommend, what in justice is due to others, to the probable detriment of that service. But when this is at any time done, we may be assured that, like a person making a confession in a Court of Justice, it is the strongest evidence adducible of the truth of what is averred. Far be it from me, however, to disparage generally the civil service of India on the ground of withholding information. The members of it have not, in general, the discrimination and application to business of Sir Henry Strachey. They never, perhaps, incline their thoughts to the contemplation of any picture adverse to their own interests and increase of emolument; although, if they should at any time do so, they are honourable enough to communicate their sentiments. And it is natural that they should indulge only pleasing prospects of their own advantage, in preference to contemplating the reverse. Little blame is therefore attributable to them for following a natural impulse, rendered the more irresistible and engrossing from the constitution of their body, by which they advance in progression through greater and greater degrees of indolence, horse-racing, and idleness, to greater and greater emolument, rank, and power. Why the Court of Directors and the Board of Control should not have discovered the value and wisdom of Sir Henry Strachey's recommendations, carrying on their face conviction of their worth and justice, it may be no business of mine to inquire. But let his Majesty's Government ascertain the reason; the poor Hindoo expects that it will, for probably no other power can. Whether it was patronage and provision for the sons of relations and friends that clogged the exercise of the understandings of the managers of India; whether it was the state policy of England, the Munro system of keeping the people down, that influenced their rejection of such sound opinions; it behoves ministers to make amends for the neglect, and to adopt such a course for the future as will do honour to their humanity and wisdom.

On the 10th of February, 1805, three years after he had communicated to the Bengal Government the sentiments I have quoted, Sir Henry Strachey, when touching on the same subject, says, "The minds of the Zemindaurs

" in general, I believe to be alienated and estranged from us; and if they forbear to rise against us and join our enemies, it is, I conceive, only because they see that our army is irresistible, and our power firmly established." ——" With respect to the possibility of restraining men from joining rebellious chiefs who can pay them, or prevailing upon dependents to detach themselves from their masters, I think it out of the question. Neither the hope of reward, nor the fear of punishment, as held out by Government, have much effect. Our influence scarcely extends to induce the servants and connexions of the most worthless outcast of a *decoit*, or assassin, to betray or desert him."——" It is not possible that a system which tends to diminish the importance of the leading men of the country, and does, in fact, encroach on their just and long established privileges, can be introduced without extreme dissatisfaction. That dissatisfaction, however, I do not mean to state as universal among the Zemindaurs. The weak, the moderate, and the peaceable, who were unable to maintain a degree of independence under the old Government, probably like the change." At the conclusion of his letter Sir Henry remarks, " I am very far from wishing to justify resistance to the sovereign power, or its officers. It is

" not my intention to question the wisdom and " equity of the acts of Government, nor to ad- " vance principles derogatory to the honour and " dignity of the State, nor disrespectful to its " members. It is our business to support the " established Government."

At a still more recent period, on the 5th of February, 1808, Mr. J. Stuart, then a judge of circuit, stated his sentiments in a style of candour and independence which does great credit to himself and to the government which could receive them without taking offence. He, however, retains his observations for mature consideration, until the 6th of May following, when he hands them up with these remarks: —" I am the more encouraged to take this " step (to submit the paper of the 5th of Fe- " bruary, 1808, to the Government) by finding " that I am not singular in my sentiments; but " that several gentlemen, whose talents and local " experience entitle their opinions to the greatest " weight, have countenanced my views on this " part of the subject."

The first extract to which I solicit attention, is a maxim which is peculiarly true in the circumstance of the conquest of one people by another people, who are foreigners and but little able to secure, through their own intercourse, the affection and loyalty of the conquered nation.

"The natural mode of managing men, is to "employ the agency of those, whom, from the "relation in which they stand to them, they "regard with sentiments of respect and confi-"dence." Mr. Stuart says respecting the ruin of the native gentry: "When the British first "acquired the dominion of these provinces, "they found a considerable body of what might "be called a native gentry."——"Taken as a "body they were not deficient in an acquaint-"ance with men and business; the knowledge "and elevation of sentiment which, in a certain "degree, seems always attached to the long "possession of power and affluence. Without too "much burthening our Government, we might "have reserved a considerable number of offices "for natives, upon a liberal footing of confi-"dence and emolument. These would have "been a resource to many of these families; "would have maintained them in a decent "state of respect and competency; and have "enabled them to give their children an edu-"cation which would have preserved them from "falling below the place which their parents "had held in society. But our Government "has not appeared to think this object worthy "their attention. If, therefore, not the policy, "it has at least been the tendency of the "internal measures of Government, to hasten "the extinction of this class of men. Accordingly, the greatest part of these families have sunk under neglect and poverty, and their descendants have become confounded with the mass of the people."——"And is it not at length time to consider what may be the influence of these principles on the character and morality of the community? As we proceed, these provinces will soon present the singular spectacle of a great empire, the Government of which rigidly excludes its subjects from every object of fair ambition, which in the pursuit could stimulate men to cultivate their faculties, or in the possession, enlarge their understandings and elevate their minds. The natives may accumulate wealth as merchants; they may be proprietors of land; but these occupations, as they are managed in this country, have no great tendency to raise the character. Beyond them, with the rarest exceptions, there is nothing to which the people can aspire, higher than the command of a platoon of sepoys, or the possession of some petty civil office, insignificant in its functions, and paid with a salary hardly adequate to a bare subsistence. My speculations may have perhaps misled me, but I am persuaded that very unfavourable effects from these causes may already be traced in the "habits of our native subjects; and their long "continuance must, I think, infallibly end in "reducing the whole population to one ignorant, "grovelling, litigious, and profligate herd.—— "Then, after the lapse of a few years, a native "of education and character will be a phenomenon; and if afterwards this consequence "should be regretted, that which might easily "have been prevented will never be retrieved."

From these unvarnished descriptions it may be inferred how far the just maxim advocated by Sir Thomas Munro, in his letter to Mr. Petrie, dated the 25th of August, 1805, has been observed, either in the Madras or Bengal Presidencies. "When a country," says Sir Thomas, "falls under the dominion of a foreign power, "it is usually found to be the wisest plan to "leave it in possession of its own laws and "customs, and to endeavour rather to ameliorate than to abolish them and substitute "others in their room; and, the more antient "and civilized the subjected nation is, the more "requisite is it to pursue this course; for the "institutions of such a people are not only in "themselves perhaps better adapted than any "that they could receive from strangers to their "own circumstances and habits, but they have "also over their minds the strong influence "which is derived from respect to antiquity."

Mr. H. Colebrook, in his Minute, dated in June, 1808, says, "It is of the utmost importance, it is essential for the safety of the State, "to conciliate the great body of the landed proprietors; to attach to the British Government "that class of persons, whose influence is most "permanent and most extensive: to render it "their palpable interest to uphold the permanence of the British domination, to give them "a valuable stake in the present administration "of the country."

I have now laid before the public, in my own language, and in that of other men, a view of the effects, on the state of society in India, resulting from the revenue and judicial arrangements adopted by his Majesty's servants, and from the substitution of a foreign for a native Government. It will be perceived that on one side are ranged Sir Thomas Munro and the advocates of his system, and Mr. Mill, the historian, in favour of reducing the inhabitants to poor agriculturists; the former, because they considered that the safest condition they could be in for the permanence of our Government; the latter, because the greatest portion of happiness would, he believed, be enjoyed by the greatest number. On the other side are also many men of eminent talents, with equal discrimination and nearly as much practical knowledge as Sir Thomas Munro. They possess over him and his supporters, however, one obvious advantage, when balanced against each other as authorities—they had no scheme of their own to advance—they merely described and reasoned on what they witnessed, and recommended to the State to devise its own plans to meet their general views. In such discussions as I have brought under review, the authority of one man will be as good as that of another, having equal advantages of information and equal discrimination and judgment. The scale will instantly turn, however, in favour of the views and information of those, who have no particular object, and from whom their sentiments were not only, as it were, drawn out, but who submitted them to their governments with doubts as to the temper with which they might be received. That the gentlemen, from whose papers I have quoted extracts, had not an equal advantage, from length of service, with Sir Thomas Munro, is true; and it may, therefore, by some, be deemed proper that both the Directors and the Board of Control should give to his opinions more credit than to theirs; but it was on this account the more necessary that, for the information of the public, I should examine them with greater strictness. Although Sir Thomas Munro may have possessed more intelligence than some; more application and intensity of attention than others; and more means and opportunities of acquiring local information than certain others; he did not, nevertheless, possess *all* those qualities and circumstances adapted for gaining correct views of things, in a superior, or even in an equal degree, to all others his contemporaries. Some had more acute discrimination and greater intelligence, though less experience, or application; others more experience, though they were less capable of taking general and just views; and so on. To admit therefore that what Sir Thomas Munro says must be true and worthy of adoption, and that what other persons individually or collectively say is erroneous, if it differs from Sir Thomas Munro's dicta, is to fetter our judgments in the discovery of new views, and of the truth respecting India. If his Majesty's Government is pleased to assume that it is not incumbent on the British nation to rule India, in such a manner as to advance the people to the greatest degree of knowledge and prosperity which it lies in our power to confer on them, then, the continuance of Sir Thomas Munro's plan is suited to the proof of their political proposition or axiom. But if we set out from a maxim the very reverse of what I have supposed, then, as it would be impossible to prove two opposite propositions by the same reasoning, Sir Thomas Munro's plan, if continued, is not suited for effecting the prosperity and increase in knowledge and civilization of the people. The pretensions of Sir Thomas Munro, to maintaining by his plans "*the institutions*" of Indian society, ought to be judged of by what others have written respecting the amelioration of the condition of Polygaurs, Zemindaurs, and others, the local gentry, as well as from what he himself has urged, not only in favour of their abolition, but against their creation or continuance.

After what I have stated, it must be needless to enlarge on the other proofs that are on record, of the people of India having, in general, retrograded in prosperity in consequence of our acquisition of their country. It is possible that I may be in error as to the causes; but the effects cannot be mistaken. The people are indisputably reduced to a very low condition of human nature; their natural chiefs have disappeared, and no object of ambition is left for their attainment. "Rewards, the great spring "of human action, are excluded from the "scheme of our internal policy. When we kill, "it is by stifling."

I might here drop the subject, satisfied that, having described the condition of the people, and obtruded my opinions of the past and present management of India, his Majesty and his ministers might devise a plan for securing the prosperity of the millions it contains, without much assistance from other persons; and it is indeed, generally speaking, true of politics as of medicine, that, when the cause of a distemper is discovered, it is not difficult to apply a suitable remedy. But, in regard to a foreign nation, to which we are desirous of preserving its own peculiar customs and laws, at the same time that we may "gradually and cautiously insinuate" wholesome innovations and reforms, it will be found that a consultation of physicians is required to examine the evidence of those who have seen and studied the patient in his paroxysms; and to determine, at least, the most palatable vehicle for the administration of whatever remedy is at length provided. I am no schemer: and my opinions on this important question are offered with becoming diffidence. Let Government consult eminent men of all classes who have been employed in Indian affairs; let it weigh and balance their opinions and recommendations; giving implicit confidence to none in particular, beyond what is challenged by their merits, *tried by the test of sound and humane principles.* The Court of Directors deserve the highest eulogium for the labour with which they have at times collected the opinions of their officers in India; but it is singular how very few of these gentlemen have taken general views of the questions put to them. Perhaps, indeed, most of them did best to furnish merely the information, and to leave it to their superiors to digest and apply it. Solicitous to see Britain perform her duty to an immense portion of the human race, grovelling in chains at her feet, and hoping that my representations may reach that high quarter which can alone give a new and accurate impulse to the exertions of the public servants; I shall proceed to submit my humble mite of advice, trusting that, though limited to general recommendations, it may have some use: and if hereafter I find that it has done any good, I may be induced to fill up the outlines of some of the more complicated considerations which the subject involves.

And here let me remark on Sir Thomas Munro, whose name I have so often mentioned in connection with his own plan, that there is no man who has so ably handled many of the important questions respecting the government of India, as he himself has done in the twenty-second and following paragraphs of that admirable and statesman-like Minute, dated the 31st of December, 1824; a paper more glorious and honourable to his character than if he had never countenanced other less worthy and valid opinions;—a paper in which he has, to a great extent, abandoned the legislating Mr. Thackeray and his sentiment, that in India are wanted only industrious husbandmen. This valuable document deserves the most deliberate attention of the Sovereign and his ministers. Were I to quote from it at all, I should extract a very great portion of it. Coming from Sir Thomas Munro's school, and from the lion himself, it carries with it a tenfold power of conviction of the propriety of pursuing that policy which I have been endeavouring to explain and recommend. This distinguished public officer has, I believe, been the first Indian Governor (Mr. Elphinstone, and he, at least, divide the honour between them) to lead the way in a liberal and just course of policy towards the natives of India, after he calculated and foresaw that our political existence is in little or no less danger from the people of that country reduced to bondsmen, than it would be were we to confer on them many of the benefits we have it in our power to bestow. His abundant humanity and benevolence had now made him eager to suggest and adopt whatever he saw would tend to the melioration of so many human beings; and I think it might not have been difficult, had he fortunately been still living, to convince his fine understanding that, in the unbending and universal application of the Ryotwaur scheme, he had made a great mistake. It would indeed have been satisfactory to acquire his sentiments of administering the revenue-affairs of India, agreeably to views unshackled by the pledge by which he seems to have bound himself to support the Ryotwaur system. But there still remain many eminent and experienced men, whom his Majesty's ministers may consult. In the first rank are the sound and intelligent Sir Henry Strachey; the magnanimous, the just, the virtuous, Elphinstone, a gentleman whose views as a statesman, and whose conduct as a man, are stamped with the most admirable wisdom and kingly liberality. Let them be consulted. There are also Sir John Stuart, Lord William Bentinck, Mr. Colebrook, and a host, I may say, of others but little their inferiors, all well informed on Indian affairs, who have the ability and knowledge requisite to furnish solid and wise opinions. I had almost forgotten to mention Sir John Malcolm; but that gentleman has talked and written so much, that his own is perhaps the only eulogium or recommendation of which he may be ambitious.

The first point that should be clearly determined is, the policy to be pursued. Is it or is it not the intention of Government to advance the nations of India to as high a step of civilization as is consistent with the maintenance of our political supremacy? I shall suppose that his Majesty's ministers do intend that their measures shall be suited to that end; and that they consider with me the following observations of Lord Bacon, peculiarly applicable to India. "The "matter of seditions is of two kinds, much "poverty, and much discontentment. It is certain so many overthrown estates are so many "votes for troubles. Lucan noteth well the "state of Rome before the Civil War,

> " 'Hinc usura vorax, rupidumque in tempore fœnus,
> " 'Hinc concussa fides, et multis utile bellum.'

"This same 'multis utile bellum' is an assured "and infallible sign of a state disposed to seditions and troubles; and if this poverty and "broken estate in the better sort be joined with "a want and necessity in the mean people, the "danger is imminent and great; for the rebellions of the belly are the worst."——"Let "no prince measure the danger of discontentments by this, whether they be just or unjust: "for that were to imagine people to be too reasonable, who do often spurn at their own good." This philosopher also says, "The surest way to "prevent seditions (if the times do bear it) is to "take away the matter of them, for if there be "fuel prepared, it is hard to tell whence the "spark shall come that shall set it on fire."

I shall then suppose that the object is to civilize the people of India, and in such a manner as, during the execution of the design, to secure our own supremacy unimpaired. And here let me protest against the specious maxims of some politicians, who would scare us with propositions about the necessity there is for abandoning the application of general truths and maxims to so singular a race of men as the inhabitants of India. What is true in Europe is true in Asia also. How cautiously soever we may proceed, it is undeniably true that we ought to work with the best instruments and materials here, as elsewhere, if we wish to make perfect our design. Cautiously acting upon true principles we are certain of success. Timorously and foolishly adopting expedients and palliatives, we may cover defects and diseases, but we shall never cure or eradicate them.

If the question were simply to civilize a people who had no institutions of their own, it could very easily be solved. But, in this case, we have not a block of marble to shape into any figure we please, but a ready-formed image badly sculptured to mould and polish, with the consent of hosts of jealous guardians, so as that it shall attain a high degree of beauty. We should first ascertain what there is of good in the institutions and manners of the people, and what there is of bad. We ought to retain all that is good, and project plans for reforming what is bad. But these plans ought to be cautiously executed. Reforms must be insinuated, not insisted upon; otherwise the open hostility of those to be reformed will be the certain result. Our wisdom and firmness must be led blindfold by conciliation. If we advance a step without that guide, we shall be entangled in a labyrinth, or fall into a pit, from which all our wisdom will never extricate us. Taking the natives along with us, they will voluntarily work with our implements, and complete our design. Advancing without their concurrence, they will deprive us of the means, and probably destroy us for our attempt to benefit them. These cases are of course put in the extreme, but, knowing the best and the worst, we shall at least act with moderation and judgment. It is truly said by Lord Bacon that "it is the solecism of power to think to command the end, yet not to endure the means."

The natives, especially of the higher castes of Hindoos, and the Mahomedans, are eager to acquire learning. Their own, of course, they esteem and prefer, but they are now daily becoming more desirous, particularly Bramins, Kayets, Prabhoos, and Sonars, of learning what we know, and of fitting themselves to serve us by an acquaintance with our language and literature. They have seen us subdue their monarchies as if by a magical feat. They fully understand that we have effected the conquest by our wisdom, valour, and prudence; and that by our unanimity and subordination we shall maintain our authority. They appreciate our intentions of being just to all men, and wonder at our moderation, inasmuch as, being their masters, and devoid of any fellow-feeling towards them but as human beings, we never oppress them. But they dislike us; they hate us as foreigners, and conquerors, and eaters of beef; the Bramins especially, who feel that their consequence and power are fast decaying. The superstitions of the lower orders are not the less gross and disgusting, though they are persevered in without so much reverence as before for the priesthood. Their morals are becoming every day worse, for there is every day a diminution of the checks to immorality that existed in the ability of the Bramins, and in the respect paid to their enforcement of moral and religious precepts. Without untying a single cord with our hands, our presence and toleration alone have loosened some of the strongest bands that united the Hindoo communities. Equal justice has engendered a contempt of superiors. Government and its magistrates take little interest, and seldom interfere in the punishment of moral delinquencies. Our refusal to arbitrate in religious and caste disputes has produced many new and given fresh life to many old ones. Low castes begin to presume on stepping beyond their line, and on adopting the usages of higher castes, even those of the Braminical order. We have either broken down or very much depressed the influence of the natural chiefs of the people by positive enactments, or through the silent operation of our levelling systems. The religious heads and learned men are, from want of encouragement, and from the spirit of encroachment on caste, fast descending into contempt and diminishing in numbers. With these facts before us, we should shape our proceedings so as to prevent the calamities the approach of which they portend. We are presented with one or two alternatives. We must either prop up a religion and a system of moral responsibility, the best parts of which are tumbling down, or we must allow them to crumble away altogether, and, by placing education and a better system within the reach of the people, draw them into morality and subordination through the conviction of their beauty and propriety. Though eminent men have considered the strength of our Government to consist in the division of the Hindoos into castes, and their consequent disunion on all points unconnected with the Hindoo religion—a disunion by the by which may be chimerical—I am inclined to view the danger of our present condition as in no degree less than it would be, were all the natives reduced to one class, provided they were treated as men, and not bound down like wild beasts or slaves. Guided by my experience of the people I should say, that leaders alone are required to unite myriads against us. Men of the lowest castes sit on the thrones to which they have raised themselves by their talents and military prowess in India, as elsewhere; and Bramins administer their affairs. I never knew caste to be an obstacle to Hindoos coalescing in any great, or even in any petty, design. It is quite true, however, that to tamper with their religion would instantly unite them in a league which might never otherwise have been formed. Sir Henry Strachey's opinion was just, for the time, but it does not hold to any extent of time. "The "total want of energy and spirit, the poverty "and ignorance, of the people, compose, in my "opinion, the strength of our Government." A bold leader, a few intelligent followers, might infuse spirit and knowledge sufficient to harass us with thousands of ignorant and barbarous foes. As for the rest, we may trust to Lord Bacon's opinion, that poverty and discontent are likely enough to generate such characters. It remains for his Majesty's Government to make an election between the only two courses left to their option; for I cannot, for an instant, entertain the belief that they would rather see the Hindoos in the most degraded state of morality, even if such a state were not highly dangerous to our supremacy in India, than (if need were to choose that course) prop up and regenerate Hindooism to a certain extent.

I shall suppose it possible that his Majesty and his advisers may agree with me in thinking, that of the two alternatives to which I have adverted, that which will afford to the natives of India opportunity to study our literature and wisdom, in the room of their own, will be the one resorted to. We should, therefore, without loss of time, encourage and gratify the taste of the Bramins and others for becoming acquainted with our stores of learning and science, by instituting royal seminaries and establishments for instructing the people, and by translating into their own languages the works of our most approved authors. The most scrupulous care should be taken to avoid every allusion to religious principles and doctrines of sects, whether Christian, Chinese, Mahomedan, or Hindoo; for if an alarm should be taken, or a prejudice imbibed that the faith of the students was liable to be unsettled, not a Bramin would send his son to be instructed. Moral precepts of every nation, whether from our own sacred book, or from the works of philosophers, should be freely taught and disseminated. The Hindoos are delighted (I speak from my own knowledge of them) with moral tales and theories; but although they have many precepts of their own, they require a new stimulus to adopt them as their rule of conduct. What it is possible to accomplish by educating, with discretion, the natives of India, can scarcely be any longer pronounced a subject of speculation. Mr. Elphinstone has fully ascertained their readiness to accept the instruction we may be prepared to afford, if it does not militate against existing prejudices of religion and caste. Of all the acts of that great man, none perhaps will, in future times, redound more to his honour and wisdom, than his establishment of schools, and his exertions to disseminate knowledge by books, among the people within the influence of his government. Discerning the glorious boon he had been conferring on them in its true colours, the native chiefs and subjects of his government have perpetuated to posterity their sense of gratitude, by founding English professorships, the fruits of a large subscription of money, in his name. Might I venture to approach the throne and to exhort the advisers of his Majesty to follow the example of this wise statesman, I would hold such language as this:—Let the name of George the Fourth be hailed in all future ages, by the nations of India, as that of the enlightener of the understandings of millions! The plan is perfectly easy, and would be a royal and suitable introduction of the King of England to this race of men, who, till lately, only knew his Majesty as the Sovereign of their rulers, and in that knowledge had no mean opinion of his power. Sorry am I to add that they have now heard of his Majesty in another character. His Majesty's judges, and the barristers of their courts, have established among them the belief that the King is the rival of the Company, as they have shown themselves the rivals of the Company's governments. The singular fatuity of an institution, which exists only because the Government itself exists, declaring to the world that the acts—all the acts—of that Government and of its servants, are illegal, has been exhibited by his Majesty's courts of justice in India; and the people are left to think that his Majesty is a rival power to the Company, which will one day enter the lists, and allow of openings for the people to establish native princes again, in the course of the scramble. These men, these foolish men, found among his Majesty's judges, have shown to the still uninformed and ignorant natives of India, that it is possible their masters should want unanimity. Let his Majesty's ministers look to this. Appoint whom you please governors of the country, the Directors of Leadenhall-street, or all the fighting and gambling barristers of all the courts of England, but let their power be undisputed in the eyes of the natives. The mischiefs that have arisen, and are daily spreading, from struggles of this kind, are incalculable; and if I might propose a remedy for them, I should say—Found colleges in the different parts of India, and show the natives that his Majesty and the Company are not rival powers, but that they are his Majesty's ministerial officers in governing the country, and that his Majesty takes a deep interest in their governing it well. Establish his fame in the understandings and hearts of his subjects, and gratify the philosophers of Britain by disclosing to them a field of delight, in communicating to the nations of the East their wisdom and discoveries. Nothing has yet been done for India. Parliament may say, "Have we not sent out "British judges to introduce British laws? "And are not British judges and British laws "the greatest boon we could give?" Inquire further. Your courts of justice, so far as they furnish for Britons a trial by their own laws, are useful; but in every other respect their influence has been lamentably malign and deleterious to the interests of the British Government. Would you not deem those who could bring his Majesty's Government into contempt to be traitors to his Government? Certainly you would, if you were not otherwise convinced that the men were infatuated or mad. The effects of the boon, the only one given to the natives by his Majesty's Government in a direct form, are, notoriously, the demoralization of those whom its influence has reached. They have learned all the chicanery and shuffling, all the tricks of law and attorneys, which they could never else have heard of, without adopting one particle of the good which the law contains. Is it to be believed that the natives, even those who are successful suitors, respect Courts and Judges, or (as they give themselves out from the Bench, the only officers bearing his Majesty's high commissions in India) that they can respect the power which appoints men to administer justice to them, who are in fact deceived at almost every turn they take; who, with the best intentions, no doubt, of doing justice in their vocation, apply technicalities of law and strict rules of evidence to the plainest propositions misunderstood; and bring forth verdicts, especially if Government is one of the parties, truly laughable, but at the same time truly to be lamented? Besides, there is no jury of the people of the country to assist them in distinguishing truth from falsehood. The judges determine, in all civil cases, both the fact and the law. This practice certainly cannot be said by parliament to afford the natives a specimen, or taste, of British justice; although it no doubt teaches them British law, which is, even lawyers will admit, a totally distinct thing. I do believe that the judges intend in all cases to afford justice: but they are thwarted by their ignorance of the value of a native's oath, by their dependence on a broken reed. They are deceived by their want of knowledge of native manners; by erroneous interpretations of nice questions; by leading questions which it is hardly possible to prevent being put, from the difficulty of explaining precisely in another language the true question asked; by the awkwardness, the scruples, of some natives in giving evidence; and by the acumen of the barristers applied to all these and many more such circumstances, tending to produce doubt and confusion in the mind of the judge, for the interest of their clients. These courts are no boon to the natives of India. They are baneful to them and to Government. The Judges, being idle about six days in the week, spell over their charters and letters patent, to discover a doubtful word or phrase, to enable them to dispute lawfully, or under what they call a legal construction, the most obvious and reasonable authority of the local Governments, and to fight with the phrase, mace in hand, under his Majesty's name and for his Majesty's honour — I had almost said *disgrace.* Never were such folly and absurdity practised since the days of the dark ages, when narrow-minded men disputed about the meaning of scriptural passages. And this is the only gift that has been sent to the people of India. Establish colleges, and dispel the doubts engendered, to no small or triflingly mischievous extent, in the minds of your subjects, by the puerilities of your servants.

In colleges and schools let the natives obtain an education to fit them for holding the offices of judges and collectors of revenue. Employed in these important offices they should, for several generations at least, be rewarded for the highly able discharge of public duties, during a considerable and fixed period, with landed estates instead of pensions, and with promotion to the privileged classes.

Magisterial powers should be intrusted to respectable men, and a local gentry should be distinguished by gradations of rank, on such a plan as has been already adopted by Mr. Elphinstone, while governor of Bombay, for the Deccan. These ranks might receive appropriate denominations, instead of first, second, third, and so on, and their privileges of rank be clearly settled and defined.

Wherever there are local gentry, let them be supported and fostered; and where there are none, and it should be found feasible to create them, let them be created. It will be admitted that land, in addition to rank and privilege, is the best security for their permanence; and I should add, above all, let the custom of inheritance by primogeniture be, if practicable, introduced. In countries, where all the land belongs to Government, and yearly reverts to it from its occupants, as described by Sir Thomas Munro, Government could have no difficulty in creating such a gentry as it may desire, without infringing the rights of others. There occur to me two ways of creating landlords in such provinces; and both might be resorted to. One is, to sell the land outright, but in portions that would form estates of a fair size, neither too large nor too small: the other is, to make it over in similar portions, without any payment in money, and to render its proprietors perpetually liable to the payment of a certain fixed tax to Government. The estates should in general be of such a size, as would be fully sufficient to inspire the owners with a strong wish to leave them unbroken to their heirs, to enable them to maintain their rank and privileges, and the names of the founders of the families, by the custom of primogeniture. The Hindoos have as much pride as any people in the world. The first mode might be adopted to a less extent than the second, and might supersede, according as it might be found useful, the second mode. A body of proprietors whose land was exclusively their own, and acknowledged by Government to be so, would, *cœteris paribus*, be desirous of the permanence of our rule, since it is evident that they could not be bettered by any change. I doubt whether, at first, even if the means were in existence, many would purchase the land freed from all future imposts under such a restriction as the law of primogeniture would appear to an Hindoo. A few Musselmans might speculate more readily perhaps. But the Hindoos have sufficient discrimination to enable them soon to become convinced of the great utility, and it would gratify their family pride if they saw, in a few instances, the practical operation, of this law of inheritance. Although, generally speaking, the Hindoo law is paramount, particular families have particular laws of division of property, which, when proved in Courts of Justice, of course supersede the consideration of the more general law. In some places of Guzerat, it is customary among many families, for instance, for the eldest brother to succeed to all the property of the father, and to retain it to himself;

but it is incumbent on him to feed and clothe, in a suitable manner, his brothers and unmarried sisters, should they require him to do so.

It is a more difficult question to determine how landed proprietors of any consequence should be created in countries where the land belongs to village corporations, and petty Mirasdaurs. Where we have already broken up corporations by the application of the Ryotwaur plan, and assumed the possession of waste, and of land, the occupants of which are now no longer forthcoming, properties of the proposed magnitude might, in preference to our keeping the land ourselves, be perhaps made; although it is true that the establishment of considerable landowners by these means would, for a considerable period, injure the revenues of Government derivable from the lands at present in cultivation, to a still greater degree, probably, than if the tracts of the intended estates were to remain with Government: for the new landlords would draw off, by low rates of rent, and by other encouragements and contrivances, more extensively than Government itself does, much of the labour and capital applied to lands that would continue to remain in the management of Government. In any plan, therefore, for creating proprietors under such circumstances, these probable effects ought to meet with great consideration; and if it is found that those I have mentioned should happen, the creation of landowners should proceed gradually and slowly. Thus perhaps, in any one year there should be assigned away no more than the 30th, or some such part, of the disposable land of any given tract, not less than from eight to thirty square miles for instance, or more, according to its populousness, fertility, or other circumstances. Such land might be disposed of in either of the two modes I have already suggested, but under the proviso of inheritance by primogeniture. Some may be of opinion that restrictions on the transfer and sale of estates should be imposed; but these would defeat one of the primary objects of the creation of landlords, a *natural* and ardent desire, on their parts, to retain to themselves and descendants the advantages which the estates produce. If such a feeling does not arise of itself, it is in vain to think to produce it by force; and it would be still less wise to calculate on the affection to Government of the holders on such conditions. Perfect freedom should be allowed, and Government should not care whether estates are transferred to rich individuals, or to persons of a particular sect or caste. To increase the vanity and pride of the holders, certain privileges, or rank, should perhaps be attached to the possession by them of certain large portions of land; and these would operate on them as an adequate stimulus to frugality, and to prevent them from dissipating their substance.

Under the native Governments, when objects of state policy rendered it expedient to reward the public services of meritorious and faithful servants, Government granted portions of untenanted or waste land, even from villages where the municipal system was in full operation; and so far, an argument is bottomed on this practice, to prove the concurrent or superior right of Government to all such land. But this power was sparingly exercised; and when it was used, the deduction of the rental of such land from the Keimal, or Tunkha, or other Berij of village assessment, only proves that the particular rights and convenience of subjects were made to yield to the necessities of the State; at the same time that a suitable indemnification was afforded to them in another shape. The same expedient might still be resorted to for the same reasons; in this case, the estates should always be composed of unoccupied or waste land, and never be given from that occupied by Mirasdaurs, or Kudeem Ryots, who are paying, or not paying, rent to Government.

Independently of the strength which our Government would derive from the existence of a gentry, whose interests and permanency should be interwoven with the stability of the British supremacy, we should, by creating such a body, be performing our duty, and giving our subjects the best chance of becoming more civilized, and of benefiting by the instruction which, I trust, will be provided for them.

To maintain our power, it will be necessary to keep in our hands only a very general superintendence of revenue and judicial proceedings, but both the generals and details of political and military affairs. Native agents, performing valuable political services should be remunerated by civil honours and landed estates. Whether such agents be Hindoos, Mahomedans, or half-castes, there should be no distinction in respect to the reward. Distinguished military talent and services ought, after a long course of service, or as the case may be, to be honoured with civil rank and landed estates; and in the interim by promotions as high as the rank of Lieutenant-Colonel. The native soldiers wear our dress; they would highly prize our titles of rank. If the deserving soldier, who was to be honoured, could read and write English with perfect fluency, he might receive a commission entitling him to command all European officers of junior rank to his own, on his own establishment. If he had not these acquirements, he ought not to be rendered entitled to this consideration; but only be made independent (as far as officers usually are so from dates of commissions) of all officers of junior rank to his own. In the first case, the native warrior would rise in the list of European officers (I hope my countrymen will not object to a well educated hero, of any hue, rising among them) by regular promotion, to the rank of Lieutenant-Colonel; performing all the duties of his station the same as the other officers: and then, if he had entitled himself to a higher distinction, he should be made eligible to the ranks of civil nobility and landed property. In the second case I have supposed that the native officer should take rank and rise in a skeleton corps, formed of such individuals as himself, but continue to perform his duty with the regiment in which he had gained distinction. Well grounded objections may probably be found to carrying these plans into effect; but if they are feasible, or any more practicable scheme for attaching to us the valour and allegiance of a naturally brave people, and of completing an important link between us and them, can be devised, no time should be lost in adopting it. Pensions, the same as British officers receive, should be granted, on retiring, to those native officers not promoted to the civil lists; and a certain number of the legitimate sons of officers, who have attained the rank of Major and Lieutenant Colonel, should be admitted, if they wish, to enter the service, first as cadets, or gentlemen volunteers, for a few years, and then to become ensigns, either in the regular or skeleton corps of the service, according to their qualifications in the English language. Several regiments entirely composed of half-castes ought to form a branch of the regular army. The command of companies might be given to half-caste officers who should raise a hundred men. The officers should be allowed to rise to the rank of Lieutenant-Colonel, and then to retire after a certain number of years' service, to any country they please, receiving the pensions of their rank; but they should also be entitled for great services to promotion to the peerage of Hindoostan, and to receive estates on the same principle as Hindoo and Mahomedan servants.

I have said that natives should hold the offices of judges and collectors. English superintendents should, however, be empowered to inquire into their proceedings; for those of the Judges, in the shape of Courts of Appeal; and for those of the Collectors, by a summary investigation of complaints, and by inspecting their settlements whenever the superintendents should think fit. The ranges of such superintendents should be very extensive, on account of the nature of their duties, as well as of the expense. Collectors of revenue should have under their care tracts of country yielding not less than six lacs of rupees, and not more than twelve lacs. Native Judges ought to be posted, generally speaking, at the distance of sixty miles from each other, so that the natives could always, by two days journey, of fifteen miles or less, attend the Court without much loss of time. On such a plan, it would take about 260 Judges for all British India, and if the average of their salaries were 500 rupees a month, the expense would be about 130,000 rupees a month, or about 1,600,000 per annum. The establishment to each need not average more than 100 rupees per month for a few Gomashtas, Mehtahs or Carcoons, or Muttesiddees, and a few Peons. The whole expense would not exceed eighteen or twenty lacs of rupees a year; and one fourth of this might be redeemed by fees and stamps. But there ought to be still higher prizes for the natives in this line. These might be formed by constituting Courts of Appeal in particular cities, whose judges should also administer the judicial affairs of those cities. The sum distributed on such an account ought to be about twenty-five lacs a year; and perhaps the European superintendence of the machine might cost fifty-five lacs;—in all, one crore of rupees, or about £1,000,000 sterling, one fourth, or more, of which would be recovered in fees and stamp duties. This, or some similar plan, should be adopted. Criminal justice, for all crimes not of a trivial nature, could easily be administered by the same machinery. Juries may, without great difficulty, be gradually introduced; as we have seen by the splendid example given in Ceylon, where their institution, in 1816, has been productive of the most beneficial effects to the inhabitants and to the administration of justice in that island.*

To carry on all the detail of receiving and issuing money at particular stations, but without any controul in supervising the conduct of the native collectors, there should be an English gentleman as accountant. He would of course report the non-transmission, at the regulated periods, of cash by the collectors, to the superintendent, whose duty it would be to inquire into the causes, and to rectify whatever was wrong.

The rentals of villages left as corporations, and, in other cases, the rents payable by indivi-

* The highly beneficial change effected in the constitution and administration of the judicial code of Ceylon has produced one of the most important concessions recently made by Colonial policy to the interests of suffering humanity, and an improvement in moral views and conduct, the result of which has been an act "that all children born of slaves after the 12th of August, 1816, shall be free."

duals or families, should be, once for all, fixed on moderate and just principles. To render them invariable as well as fixed, they should bear reference to a certain quantity of produce in kind; and a comparison should be made with this standard at the end of stated periods, for a new period. Thus, instead of saying a certain village shall pay 1000 rupees per annum, its rent should be described to be the average price in twenty by-gone years (or other period) of so many Khundees of grain for the next twenty years. The value of this grain might at one period be only 900 rupees for one period of twenty years, 1000 rupees for another period, and 1100 rupees for a third. This operation would correct the effect of any alteration in the value of money, and make the tax on land as invariable, perhaps, as it is possible to render it. No improvement of the land should be taxed, unless Government be at the expense of it; and even then, after the outlay of capital is redeemed by a heavy or a light assessment on those benefiting by the improvement, Government ought thereafter to be satisfied with six or seven per cent. on the profits accruing from the undertaking. The rents of villages and of individuals may best be fixed by a survey; but a survey without any other object than to ascertain the quantity of land made over, and the quantity and situation of what remains with Government to dispose of by sale or gift. The less particular we are in ascertaining the quality of the lands, the greater chance there will be of their improvement by those owning them. It is useless to rate land on fictitious schemes of valuation; for, when we look at the beggars who are to complete the philosophical analysis by paying the quotas we have fixed, conviction flashes across the mind that we have begun at the wrong end, and ought to have solved the proposition synthetically. I am almost inclined to recommend that the Ryots should be allowed to fix their own rents in perpetuity; nor do I think Government will lose much immediately; for the utmost, probably, that a Ryot would deduct from his present rents, if the question were put to him, would not exceed a few per cent.; and he would think it hardly possible that even so much was really intended to be conceded to him. Mr. Thackeray tells us that there are many thousand mistakes, frauds, &c., in a survey assessment: and from my own experience I say he is right. We could, with much less trouble, make as many blunders, or inequalities rather, in assessing the country, and, if my reasoning is well-founded, much to the benefit of the agriculturists. These hints may serve to enable some one to strike out some such arrangement as I have advised in a better form.

It may, perhaps, be concluded that, because I disapprove of English-bred Judges for this country, I think highly of the Company's Judges; but I disclaim any such opinion. I certainly think that the Judges of the Company's Government do not commit one mistake for five made in his Majesty's Courts; but the country Judges are, the best of them, not very well skilled in their profession. There is no public mention of their proceedings; and the best stimulus to attention to his duty in a Judge in England, the exposure of his judgments, is not felt by the Company's judicial functionaries. Nevertheless, they are men, generally speaking, of plain understandings, tolerably well acquainted with the languages and customs of the people, but far from being remarkable for activity: many of them, indeed, are useless drones; although there are some whose talents and application would do honour to any service. What they especially require is, to be trained better to the knowledge of justly appreciating evidence. I have witnessed as lamentable instances of injustice in a Company's Court, from this defect in the Judges, men too of straightforward judgments on most occasions, as I have ever observed in his Majesty's Courts from other causes. It is remarkable that the Company's Judges, knowing so little professionally as most of them do, should make so few blunders; while his Majesty's Judges, who are constantly studying law and the rules of evidence, and fighting with them day and night with both hands, should make so many more than they. The Company's Government permit boys to sit on their seats of judgment. This is not only bad, but it is wicked. It is bad for Government; it is wicked as respects the natives. Sir Thomas Munro has justly said, that the European character is one of the chief pillars of our Government in India. We shall certainly shake this pillar if we trust its support to young men on the judgment-seat. It is in truth disgusting, and must greatly add to the force of the heart-burnings of a subjected people, to see a self-sufficient youth sitting to determine the sober concerns of grey-haired men, evincing the utmost impatience and petulance, and deciding on the right to property (of no small amount to those concerned) by a whim of suspicion, or from some glimpse he has acquired of one part of the evidence. The natives are sharp-sighted enough to observe that the young man's mind is seldom present with the business before him, but has wandered to where he is most commonly to be discovered himself, the stable or the drawing room. Yet would such a youth deem it a high impertinence if his superior in office were to doubt his capability of deciding causes as well as he can dock dogs, or dance waltzes. As young men will be young in their manners and conduct, let what will happen, the system by which they fill situations so unsuitable to their discretion and age should be altered. Let no suits that are original be decided by European officers; and let men be placed in Courts of Appeal, whose conduct is steady, and whose imaginations are somewhat cooled by years; who can prove their qualification for the office by displaying, on examination, a competent knowledge of the general principles of law and evidence, and of the languages and laws of the people. The rules of the civil service indeed require revision. At present, the junior members believe they have *a right* to be provided for in offices of trust, whether they are qualified to fill them or not; just as if their claims to serve in such and such places were to supersede the natural and just rights of the people to be well served, or well governed: as if it did not signify, whether their rulers were all day in dog-kennels, or in their offices; provided they were well paid for being looked at, as the persons denominated Judges. Some of these considerate rulers never allow their consciences to whisper to them that they ought to work for their salaries; and still less do they reflect on the moral delinquency, the absolute wickedness in fact, of not attending to the concerns of his Majesty's poor subjects, who can gain redress at the hands of no other persons. Let the administration of justice be given into the hands of the natives of the country, to men who will work, and secure for his Majesty's Government the gratitude of his subjects, for the enjoyment of the inestimable blessings of speedy and cheap justice; and let there be an end of this childish trifling with the feelings and properties of thousands.

Mr. Elphinstone, when Governor of Bombay, instituted a rule, which ought to be made universal. It is directly the reverse of Sir Thomas Munro's method of guessing the delinquency of the native public servants. The rule is, that the head of any office shall not dismiss the public servants of any department, without convicting them of criminality after a regular investigation; and that, if any servant shows great incapacity, the sanction of Government shall be first required to his dismissal. It is unnecessary to expatiate on the usefulness of such a rule, in affording confidence to respectable natives to enter our service. It secures them against the petulance and favouritism of new heads of offices and of young men. It saves them from losing their places, because a new master dislikes his predecessor in office, and will not even do business with his clerks.

I have only one word to say about surplus revenue being remitted to England after the Company's debt is paid. Not a farthing should be spent, or sent, out of India, until public highways are made from one end of it to another. The interchange of commodities at a cheap rate of carriage, the ease and security of travellers, and the introduction of good wheeled machines, next to the institution of colleges and the dissemination of knowledge, ought to be the first care of his Majesty's Government.

I can offer but little counsel concerning the renewal of the Charter. If India is governed so as to advance the natives in the scale of human nature, in my opinion it does not signify who are the instruments. There can be but one opinion, however, among those who know any thing of the interior of India, that, whether the Charter be renewed or not, the greatest caution should be used not to push changes, even on the best principles, too far, or too fast. The fears of Sir Thomas Munro and others, respecting an unrestrained intercourse of European traders with the natives, ran, in my judgment, too much into the extreme. But that extreme was, unquestionably, on the safe side. Although I cannot approve, therefore, these fears, or consider them as being founded on a solid basis, there are many truths in Sir Thomas's opinions on this subject: and I confess the difficulty of drawing a line that would answer the purposes of a free trade, and also avoid, for many years to come, exciting alarm among the people. England may have benefited by a free trade, but I feel assured that India has not. Much of the circulation of capital, attendant on the manufacture of the raw produce of her soil into various commodities, has been grasped by England. The traders of the mother-country buy her raw cottons for instance, and can afford to transmit them to England, to bring them back again manufactured, or only in the shape of thread, and to undersell the manufacturers of similar articles in India. In the words of Mr. Mill, "This is exactly the same sort of policy as if "Yorkshire were to be drained and oppressed "for the benefit of Middlesex." There is, no doubt, an increased demand for raw productions, and this is the whole benefit to India; — a benefit, however, by no means equal to the loss which it suffers by the ruin of its manufacturers. A few British subjects make fortunes by supplanting hordes of poor weavers, who, unable, as well from caste, as from ignorance of other arts, to adopt new lines of life, are reduced to beggary and starvation. Let no Englishman boast of riches acquired at such a price, and by so much misery. If the Charter is renewed to the Company, his Majesty's ministers ought to insist on the adoption of some plan for securing to the internal affairs of India the superintendence of men of experience and philosophers, who will view things in lights that mere men of habit, although possessed of strong understandings, would never discover. At present, this superintendence is left to blind chance, and men (I wish to speak with no disparagement of any particular persons) who have all their lives been at sea, or in agency, or banking houses, to whose turn it comes to legislate for India, must often be puzzled with very plain subjects, and trust to the clerks in their offices for answers to important questions. The clerks may be clever men enough, and may sometimes give good opinions enough; but, if their opinions are really good in most cases, they ought to be made the Directors.

In the preceding pages, I have offered, with the most perfect sincerity, my opinions and information, and if they assist his Majesty, or his ministers, in discovering the truth, in adding lustre to his throne, and benefiting the natives of India, I shall feel satisfied with myself for having undertaken the task. Let them act upon true and enlightened principles, whatever they do, but regulate their application from time to time, according to the temper of the people, to whom, and to whose affairs, they are to be applied. "If "your wine be never so good, and you are "never so liberal in bestowing it on your neigh-"bours," says Dr. Watts, "yet, if his bottle, "into which you attempt to pour it with free-"dom, has a narrow mouth, you will sooner "overset the bottle than fill it with wine." And so of his Majesty's Indian Crown; if those to whom he delegates his authority go too far, or too fast, they will inevitably occasion the loss of it.

NOTES.

A—page 41

It is to be hoped that the wise restrictions of the Bombay Government, in respect to the rates of rent of Mirasdaurs being left without increase, will be adhered to; but the worst is to be feared when such clauses as the following are left to the understandings of native assessors: "The assessment, however, of Miras land in many villages "being as vague and indefinite as that of land held by "tenants at will, it is equally requisite it should be re-"gularly classed, and its rent defined." And again:— "In many places, however, parcels of Miras land are held "at a fixed rent for the whole rent; in others, one aver-"age rate of the rent per beegah prevails, but the size of "such beegah is greater or smaller in proportion as the "land is of good or inferior quality. In others again, an "average rate per beegah prevails on the whole lands, "which are distributed according to their respective quali-"ties amongst the whole body of the Ryots, in proportion "to the number of ploughs possessed by each individual. "In *these* cases, where no classification or definite assessment "exists, it must be introduced." How Mr. Chaplin slides away into the assertions, that "*fixed rents*" for parcels of

Miras land, may be "indefinite," and that there may be a want of "a classification and definite assessment," where "*one* "*average rate* of rent per beegah prevails, the size of such "beegah being greater or smaller, *in proportion* as the land is "of good or inferior *quality*,"—could with difficulty be accounted for, if it were not known that his mind was biassed by the Ryotwaur knowledge which he had acquired under a different state of the tenure of the land. The assessor too will very probably mistake, or, it may be, do only what it is intended he should, in "introducing definite assess-"ments" for such lands of Mirasdaurs, by applying to them the scale of rent ordered for lands whose assessment is undefined. This scale is, sixty parts of the gross produce to be left with the Ryot, and forty parts to be taken by the Sircar. Notwithstanding the laudable anxiety of the Bombay Government not to tax improvements, this rule of fixing the rent by shares of produce strikes at the very root of all their other restrictions, for, if the land is thus appraised, it will be taxed according to its *actual condition*, and not according to its natural powers of production in ordinary circumstances.

B—page 44

Sir Thomas Munro, in his Minute of the 31st December, 1824, says, "If we create Zemindaurs, and turn over to "each of them some hundreds of Ryots, we should commit "a gross injustice, because we should enable the Zemin-"daurs, in time, *to degrade* the Ryots from the rank of "*tenants in chief* to that of tenants at will, and often to "that of mere cultivators or labourers." Probably, this maxim may be turned in another direction with more efficiency and truth. Why may it not be applied to our *raising* the tenants at will of existing landlords to what

Sir Thomas Munro would probably call their just position—to *tenants in chief*, occupying the waste land of the said Mirasdaurs, or existing landlords?—a levelling upwards, as it were, that might prove one of Sir Thomas Munro's dicta,—1stly, "that no Mirasdaurs exist; and, 2dly, that "if they do exist, their land is of no value;" a liberty and equality scheme (minus .the liberty, however) by which crowds of Arcadians should, every man, pay a subscription to the State, in a ratio proportionate to the value of the rags and hovel secured to him against thieves and landed proprietors.

C—page 53.

In addition to Mr. Thackeray's sentiments, those of another Ryotwarry gentleman, respecting *inequalities* of assessment producing baneful effects both on the Ryots and Government, may be here cited. In his instructions to assessors, (*Revenue Selections*, Vol. III. page 881,) Mr. Chaplin says, "The fixing the assessment of waste lands is no less "an important operation than that of defining the rent of "those that are cultivated, for *it has been found from ex-* "*perience*, that where they have been rated too low in "consequence of their being waste, the stock of the Ryots "has afterwards been transferred to them from the cul- "tivated lands, to the great detriment of the revenue."

D—page 55.

In the 14th paragraph of his Minute, dated 31st of December, 1824, Sir Thomas Munro says, "There are *many* "Ryots who fail from another cause, which *no abatement* "of assessment can remove; and which it is not desirable "should be removed; it is occasioned by a spirit of independence among the husbandmen which urges *every* "labouring servant who can buy a pair of bullocks to "quit his master, and to take land and cultivate for him-"self." But then in the 11th paragraph, he says,—"The land of the Baramahal will, probably, in time, *all* "become saleable, even under its present assessment." Now a doubt must strike every one, that, if what is stated in the first passage be true, there will be nobody to buy the land of Baramahal when it is brought to market, either *in toto*, or in patches. In the 12th paragraph of the same Minute, Sir Thomas observes—"The land in most of "the provinces under the Madras Government is occupied "by *a vast number of small proprietors, or Ryots*, hold-"ing *properties* of *every* size, from two or three, to two "or *three thousand* acres, and some few having whole vil-"lages." Is it in this passage meant to say that "*Ryot*" signifies "*proprietor*," and that the *vast mass* of the *Ryots* of the Madras Presidency are *proprietors?* What also becomes of this check to the acquisition of large properties, "As there is every where plenty of good land lying un-"cultivated, which any person may occupy on paying the "Sircar rent, *it is evident* that no Ryot will hold land of "another," &c. Again writes Sir Thomas, in the 11th paragraph of the Minute,—"But the question regarding "Meeras is one rather of *curiosity*, than of any real utility; "for in most districts, the Meeras is worth little, and has "no value that might not easily be given to the lands in "every province, by a moderate reduction in the assess-"ment." How provoking it is, that men of the finest talents should be sometimes liable to have their judgments so completely warped by prejudice, as to make such blunders as that in the above passage! When Sir Thomas Munro found existing the very class he himself wished to create, in spite, too, of Hindoo law, and of the impossibility of any individual securing an under-tenant, he tells us, the question of such a class is merely one of *curiosity*, and not of real utility. "It is *only*," he adds, "on the "Malabar Coast, that the Meeras yields such a rent as to "make it generally saleable." It is greatly to be feared that this is only too true; at least, it appears certain that land, which was *formerly*, every day, saleable in the Deccan, has, since the introduction there of the Ryotwaur system, become of no value. Sir Thomas boasts of a few fields having become Miras in Baramahal. Mr. Chaplin ought to tell us, if he could, how many Miras fields, that were at one time saleable in the Deccan, are not saleable now. Does Sir Thomas Munro mean gravely to assert, that there is no real utility in a body of Mirasdaurs, who are not of his own creation, or that they should first be destroyed; and that then, when the country, after a long lapse of time, begins to recover its energies, and one or two sales of land occur, we are authorized to exclaim:—See the landed property we have created!—See the blessings we have conferred!

E—page 60.

In the 39th paragraph of his Minute, dated the 31st December, 1824, Sir Thomas Munro appears willing to smooth off the rougher corners of some of his old opinions and as the following sentiments come from him and his school, there need be no apprehension whatever, that he has drawn too highly coloured a picture. "One "of the *greatest disadvantages* of our Government in "India, is, its tendency to lower, or destroy, the higher "ranks of society, to bring them all *too much* to one level, "and by depriving them of their former weight and in-

" fluence, to render them less useful instruments in the in-
" ternal administration of the country. The native Govern-
" ments had a class of rich gentry, composed of Jagurdaurs
" and Examdaurs, and of all the higher civil and military
" officers. These, with the principal merchants and Ryots,
" formed a large body, wealthy, or, at least, easy in their
" circumstances." Will it be doubted, therefore, that there was no "gradation of rank" among the Hindoos, before the country was conquered by Britain? or will it be doubted that, "These advantages have almost entirely ceased under "our Government?" (Minute, par. 39.) Or will it be doubted that, as we could not have great civil and military native servants, we ought to have made gentlemen in some other way? And what other so good, as by making great proprietors? Will it be said that we preserve to the people their ancient constitution and manners, when we have swept away so important a class of the society? Will it be argued for a moment that *this* was *no* innovation? Or that, being a sweeping and desolating innovation for the people, we ought to make *no other* innovation that our circumstances would permit us to make, for the *benefit* of the people, because forsooth, it would be *an innovation?* We can innovate enough, when any obstacle of custom opposes our designs, for our own good; but we must not venture to innovate for the good of the people, or to indemnify them, by a new fashioned coat, for the loss of the old one we took from them. No, no; it would hurt their feelings to offer it to them, and they would, poor ignorant fellows, rather go naked; and naked indeed they are!

F—page 66.

In some places of Guzerat, the villages have wisely combined, in order to preserve their waste land, and insisted on

Government taking their security for each other's rents; and by thus clinging to an hereditary right, to a custom which they saw we should readily concede to secure the revenue, they have endeavoured to maintain their really valuable rights in the waste land. This is the subterfuge of the weak against the strong; but Government never, it is said, uses its subjects "as the strong usually deal with the weak."—No—proprietary Zemindaurs alone could do that, and show even that the Government in comparison with them is also weak.

G—page 70.

In Sir Thomas Munro's Minute, dated the 31st of December, 1824, he says, "The waste in Meeras villages in "Arcot is supposed by Mr. Ellis to belong to the Meerasdaurs "jointly; and he supports his opinion by documents showing "that, when a Meerasdaur sells his cultivated lands, he "transfers, by the same deed, to the purchaser his right "in the produce of the waste, the quarries, mines, fisheries, "&c., within the limits of the village. But this appears to "be a mere technical form, which can give no actual pro-"prietary right in the waste. It is used in villages where "there is no waste, as well as where there is, and may be "used where there is no Meeras. It confers a right, but not "the right of ownership, to the pasture of the waste lands, "and the fishery of the tanks and nullahs, in common with "the other Meerasdaurs of the village. The same right "exists every where. In those parts of the Deccan where "Meeras is unknown, the Ryots of every village reserve "the fishery and pasture to themselves, and drive away the "cattle of strangers," &c. Let this passage be compared with the maxim of the English Lawyers,—"By a grant of "*the profits* of the land, the *whole land* doth pass. For

" what is land but the profits thereof?" Sir Thomas says, "Mr. Ellis supposes;" but Mr. Ellis *proves by documents.* Sir Thomas says, " but this appears to be a mere *technical* "form:" the fact of the existence of such forms and such rights is indisputable, but by an Indian figure of rhetoric, we are told that they are *technical;* that they have no meaning in them; that they are mere deceptions; a sort of *mirage* that deceives the understandings of Englishmen in India! We should want a Sir Thomas Munro at every bar of every Court of Justice in India, to explain what parts of bonds are technical, and what are real, if we give the slightest credence to such assertions. But every person who knows India well, knows also that there are no technicalities, no legal fictions, no John Does and Richard Roes, in the primitive, sensible, and yet (as to matter) precise and formal deeds, and documents of the people.

If this technicality is used in regard to villages where there is no waste at the time, it simply means that if there should be any waste at any future time, he or they receiving the deed are to become entitled to the previous owner's rights in it. If a man buy a cow giving no milk, and she should afterwards give milk, Sir Thomas would say, perhaps, it was a mere technical proceeding on the part of the cow for the benefit of Government. Sir Thomas says, " *it may* " be used in villages where there are no Meerasdaurs. This exactly proves the existence of village "municipalities" where there are no Meerasdaurs; and that Sir Thomas Munro has mistaken a cause for an effect. Sir Thomas Munro also says, " The *right* of the Ryots to the waste is only good against " *strangers,* but *not* against *the Government.*" But it will be difficult to explain what use, in a thousand out of a thousand and one cases, Government could make of it, if it took it from the village, and did not transfer it *to strangers.* He says, " he thinks there is, by the usage of "the country possessed by Government, the *absolute* right "of disposing of the waste as it pleases, in villages which "are Meeras, as well as in those which are not. In the "Deccan, in Meeras villages, *the corporation has not* the "right of disposing of unoccupied land, *but the Sircar has.*" We are referred for the proof of the last assertion so boldly advanced under the great authority of Sir Thomas Munro, to Mr. Chaplin's Report on the Deccan, dated 20th August, 1822. But Mr. Chaplin is one of the strongest advocates of Sir Thomas Munro's system, and was as much pledged as his principal to defend such an argument; for, if the Ryotwaur advocates are driven from this key of their position—if they are worsted in this question about waste land—the injustice of their plans would be exposed. No prudent advocate of the system, therefore, will ever acknowledge the strongest documentary evidence to weigh any thing against his own simple assertions, unsupported by any sort of proof. What else can be said of Mr. Chaplin at least, who, as he could not deny the facts, shuffles over all the documentary proof of the very reverse of his dictum, which was adduced by the collector of Poona, and submitted to Government by Mr. Chaplin, apparently in the very same dispatch in which he hazards his unwarranted conclusion! Mr. Robertson has proved from undoubted evidence that the Paishwa, the despotic sovereign of the Deccan, had, only a few years before he was overthrown, purchased waste land (or ghutkool, as it is called in the Deccan) from the bodies corporate of villages in his own dominions, for his own private use. The Bombay Government adopted Mr. Chaplin's sentiments on this point, but with some reservation. "In "Poona and Ahmednuggur, a right is supposed to exist in the "villagers to all ghutkool, i. e. Meeras, that has lapsed from "the death or absence of the Meerasdaur, but it is incom- "patible with the existing rights of Government to dispose "of it; and it would be unwise to allow that right to be "compromised under the existing rules of assessment (viz. "the Ryotwaur rules). Though the extension of the Mee- "ras tenure be desirable, the unqualified admission of the "pretended right of these villagers might frustrate that "object." (*Rev. Select.* Vol. III. pages 809 and 810.) Sir Thomas says, *the right of the Government is absolute.* The Bombay Government, more moderate, and not bound to defend such an argument through thick and thin, only say, *the unqualified* admission of the *right to it of the villagers* (not that of the Government it will be observed) would be improper: yet there is much that might have been better in the sentiments of this Government. It designates that right, a *pretended* right, which had been recognized by a former monarch of the country, by the very fountain of law and justice at the time, by a despotic prince who would never have dreamt of paying a sum of money for what he could have had for nothing, had he not been acted upon by his desire to do what was just in a matter of right and previous custom. The Government has staggered sideways into Mr. Chaplin's road, probably because it could do no otherwise, "under the existing rules of assessment." The instances adduced of the sale of such lands to private persons are numerous; and who will doubt, or say, that our usurpation of the waste land is not as great an innovation in respect to the lower orders, as our conquest of the country was to the higher? Let them come forth, and they will be met by those who will bury them and their assertions under mountains of undeniable proofs.